WRESTLING
WITH GOD

BY RICK DIAMOND

Relevant Books

Published by Relevant Books
A division of Relevant Media Group, Inc.

www.relevantbooks.com
www.relevantmediagroup.com

Cover Design: Raul Justiniano
Interior Design: Danny Jones
Relevant Solutions
www.relevant-solutions.com

For information:
RELEVANT MEDIA GROUP, INC.
100 South Lake Destiny Dr. Ste 200
Orlando, FL 32810
321-206-8844

For bulk orders, call 800.283.8494.

Library of Congress Control Number: 2003090302
International Standard Book Number: 0-9714576-7-0

05 06 07 9 8 7 6 5 4 3

Printed in the United States of America

To my wife, Leslie, whose support of me, personal integrity, and dedication to her own walk with Christ have been my inspiration and encouragement. And to Chet Thomas, a true man of God, whose vision began the process by which this book came to be.

ACKNOWLEDGMENTS

Thank you to my family, Leslie, Alex, and Caitlin, simply because you're the best things in my life, and I'm so grateful that I get to be part of yours. You are amazing human beings. And thanks to Olivia.

I also thank the people of Riverbend Church, especially Pat Abbott, Stacie, and the entire staff. The past year and a half has been the most gratifying experience of my career, and I thank God every day that the Spirit worked it out so that we could be in ministry together. And a special thanks goes to Dr. Gerald Mann, whose vision and courage birthed this wonderful place. Grace matters.

To Cameron Strang at Relevant Media Group, I'm so glad that we listened to God speaking, and emailed, and had that phone call—what a great opportunity you've given me. I believe so strongly in the work you're doing through Relevant Media Group and thank you for your leadership. You're an inspiration to me about what the Kingdom can become in the twenty-first century. Cara, my editor, and Erika, her brave sidekick, thank you so much for your help and willingness to push me and make the book as strong as it could be. Great job.

I love and thank the Teagues, the Rakes, the Severns, R1, Sandra and Miles, the Ward's Boys, the Bubbas, the beloved Lakeview Gang!, Reflections, Couples With Kids, Into The Word, Pollard U.M.C., Drew and the D. Min. folks, Drew at 101X, Dan Jones, Anne Lamott, Richard Rohr, C. S. Lewis, and, of course, U2.

Come, Holy Spirit, fill the hearts of your faithful, and kindle in them the fire of your love. Send forth your Spirit, they shall be created, and you shall renew the face of the earth.

-*Rick Diamond*

INTRODUCTION

This book is about the spiritual journey. Specifically, it has been guided by my own walk with God, which is strange and amazing and wonderful, and by my discussions and sharing with a few hundred other travelers along the paths. I've also been guided in my thinking by the writings and insights of the pilgrims who were here ahead of us—the Christian mystics, the saints, and the great fathers and mothers of the faith. And I'm also led by my own skepticism and my own awareness of how big the world and God are, and how small religion is.

I don't know where you are, whether you're a Christian or not, whether you believe in or have rejected religion, whether you know God or don't. But for me, I'm deeply distrustful of and unimpressed by organized Christian religion. Part of that is because I was raised in three different denominations, and my walk was punctuated by disappointments and frustrations. Part of why I'm that way is because I've worked in religious settings for the past decade. And part of my distrust is because I have studied the way churches work and have worked through the centuries. The Church has done great good, encouraged moral behavior and charity, and has done its best to point people to what it has understood about God. And yet, the Church is often—maybe even usually—corrupt, self-serving, and mostly concerned about defending its own boundaries and safety. It has hurt people in countless ways, either through its own sickness and dysfunction, or simply by setting the standard way too low for what people could become if God were given some room. In some ways, it's not Christianity's fault; it's made up of people, like anything else, and people are broken and dysfunctional. To be a healthy person, you understand, have compassion, and move on. But some days you think, "You guys say you're the ones who know the ultimate truth, and you're arguing over really stupid things. Get over it."

And yet, even with all of the brokenness of the Church overall, I'm always hopeful about what Jesus called The Kingdom of God, which is the work that God's Spirit does all the time—and the transformation that can happen when the Spirit is allowed to breathe. God's persistence and hopefulness amaze me and tell me to continue to believe in things I thought weren't possible. And it's important to make the distinction that the Kingdom of God is much, much bigger than the Christian Church. God is in all of creation, all of that mysterious stuff out there we don't even know the first thing about or understand, working in all of human history. God isn't restricted by our denominations or definitions. God is the "other" that we're longing for—and that God is very real and very present, regardless of how small we've attempted to make Him. So the work I do, and what I hope I'm doing in this book, is looking forward, past religious experience or denominational doctrine. Those boxes are too small to put God in.

I can't begin to fathom anything for sure about what God is. What I am convinced of is that there is someone who is larger than everyday human experience, someone who wants to know me, someone who is already present with me. I think that's what the real heart of being a follower of Christ has always been about. So that's what I wish for you. I hope that your life will be made more meaningful because you are curious, listening, feeling; I believe that what you'll find is God's love. It takes effort and openness to let love happen in us. We're not great at it. But love is persistent and doesn't give up easily. That's why this book is about wrestling.

So may God's love go with you on your journey. Wait—that's not right. May you find that God's love has always been and will always be there, right where you are at this moment, and may you become a person who knows he or she is God's beloved.

-Rick Diamond

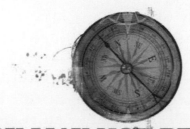

YOU MAY NOT BE SURE
WHERE, BUT YOU'RE HERE

CHAPTER_ **1**

I'm having a conversation with a friend, Janice, in a coffee shop. We're talking about mutual friends, music, movies, and life. She slowly proposes a question, thinking through it as she asks.

"How do you know that what you believe is really true? How do you know what they've been telling us all these years isn't just something someone made up?" She isn't really asking me to answer. She's thinking.

"My grandparents thought that there was a clear answer for every single question, and that some things were just true because they'd always been true. We were supposed to respect our elders, and be nice, and go to school. We were supposed to become these little productive members of society."

I know what she's talking about: the sweet families on television, the rules of behavior and morality drilled into our heads through sheer repetition at school and church [and the shame if we didn't obey], and the belief in America, the flag, God, and goodness.

"It's crap," Janice says. "My father is this successful lawyer and church member and respected figure, and the whole time—my whole life—he's this person who lies and cheats behind the scenes to get what he wants. He belittles my mother. He's not there for me or my sister. He's emotionally dead." She's a mixture now of anger and grief and determination. Her eyes narrow.

"I don't ever want to be like that," she says. She sticks her fork into the leftover crust of her cinnamon roll. "I want to really be who I am and tell the truth." She's not done.

"And another thing," she says, glancing into the street and then back at me, still determined. "Is it possible to be a lot of things at once? Like, many faiths, or no faith, but something you just believe inside? Part of one or two religions, but part of you is no religion? Like, I really love the meditation that I do with my friend Darla at the Zen center downtown, and they never taught us that in Sunday school when I was a kid. So does that mean that if I do yoga or read Buddha's teachings, I can't know Jesus either?

"And is it possible that God isn't contained in religion at all?" Now Janice is shifting in her chair. She's anxious.

"There's a part of me that's sort of excited when I think that—and a part of me that wonders if I'm going to hell. But I'm not sure what to do about that. Am I going to hell?"

I tell her that I don't think for a second that she is.

"I don't think so either." And she adds, "But don't tell my mother what I've been saying just now."

She laughs. I do too.

I think this place Janice has traveled to is part of where we all are in the twenty-first century. We're not all in the same place. But millions of us have inherited similar contexts. And it's a bit of a mess.

It's hard for the people who've been raised since the American cultural revolutions of the last fifty years to believe that something at the macro level isn't just basically screwed up. What we seem to have ended up with is a multiple-personality culture. And it's not one side versus the other, like Democrat and Republican; it's dozens of sides, parts, and splinters all going in different directions at once, some overlapping and some universes away from each other.

We don't all agree about where we are, much less where to go from here in the decades to come.

We want to trust something, but what we've ended up with is a strange disconnection with everything that was true before we came along. The institutions and systems our grandparents knew are outdated and too simple for most of us to believe in; the reforms and revolutions our parents' generation were raised through tore down so much that sometimes it seems as if there's little left that won't fall over any minute, if it hasn't collapsed already. U2 sings a song that begins, *Jesus, Jesus can you hear me? | I'm alone in this world, and a f---ed up world it is, too.*[1] But Bono also sings, *It's a beautiful day.*[2]

3

[1] U2, Bono and The Edge, lyrics, "Wake Up Dead Man," *Pop*, c1997 Polygram International Music Publishing B. V., Island Records, Inc., 314-514-334-
[2] U2, Bono and The Edge, lyrics, "Beautiful Day," *All That You Can't Leave Behind*, PolyGram International Music Publishing B. V.; c2000 Universal International Music B. V., Interscope Records 314-524-653-2.

We hope that bad things won't happen and that all will be well, like on *Friends,* where every problem is funny, and all conflicts get resolved in thirty minutes, or, at the most, a two-part episode. But you know that real life isn't like that. Buses crash. Children are snatched from their front yards. Presidents resign in disgrace or maintain their addictions, like lots of other people we know. It occurs to us after a while that this isn't anything new.

We understand that there's a great deal of goodness around us, and yet we also have to acknowledge that there's a lot of junk. Our parents and grand-parents love us, but even the very best of them don't belong on, say, a sentimental camera commercial. They're flawed. Nobody on a camera commercial ever goes to the bathroom or hits their wife, for example. We're surrounded by suburban Goths, skeptical patriots, spiritual beings who are also cynical. That's this culture.

Shrek is a lot like us: we believe in the hopefulness of the fairy tale and the love story, but we also like that it's irreverent and admits that life isn't all sweetness. *Shrek* starts in an outhouse and ends in an onion, but it's an onion wedding carriage. That makes sense. True love in a big onion.

The life we're constructing now isn't safe or perfect, but it's what we know. And we try to be honest about what we've got to work with. It's like a situation comedy but one where a guy stands offstage with a machine gun.

We fantasize that we're like the models, or the movie stars, or the sports heroes. That someday we'll be on *Survivor* or *American Idol.* That getting up, going to school or work, hanging out with friends, is enough. Go shopping. Read. Run. And it's good. It's fine. To make that life more pleasant, we buy more toys—music, entertainment centers, sports equipment, cars, houses, cigarettes, vacations, power, stuff, more channels. And we spend some time there for a while. It's fun. But we also can tell that we're not *building* anything. Which is okay on the short run. And right now feels like the short run. No hurry yet.

Some days, though, we feel a little like Edward Norton in *Fight Club*. We've filled our apartment with great and beautiful crap from upscale catalogs and malls, but there is a yawning black hole in our head. In his case, he responds with violence and schizophrenia. But surely that's not necessarily the only alternative. We can do both, right? Balance between getting stuff and enjoying life, and also waiting to see if anything more *lasting* comes up.

So we keep looking for "it." Most days, we find ourselves just doing life. And that's really, honestly, enough for right now. And, seriously, that's okay. But at the same time, all along, you may be like me. I keep listening, at least a little here and there, for something behind or below the noise of my everyday life.

I'm not cynical or checked out. I am passionate about the things that matter to me. I believe in some things. They may not be the things my parents want me to care about or commit to, necessarily, but they're mine. It's not that I'm refusing to cooperate with what they value or that I absolutely refuse to continue the progress that came before me; it's just that they didn't leave us much solid building materials to work with. But just because this is the most diverse and open culture in the history of Western civilization, and it appears that every question is now fair to ask, doesn't mean that nothing matters to anyone who's not signed up yet. It's that we want something to belong to that actually does matter. And we'll wait and see, and in the meantime, keep going.

I think maybe that's a good name for this way of living. It's about waiting expectantly but not desperately. A "we'll see" mind. We haven't ever known anything but the weird, chaotic mixture of hopefulness and realism of the postmodern world. We're curious, but not desperate. We're not motivated by guilt or fear; we're too jaded for that. So we wait. But we're not passive. Real waiting and seeing is active. It takes a watching and listening heart.

A lot of us have parents and institutions around us, and voices within us, that want us to decide what we believe, or who we're going to be, and commit to something. But what? And why do I have to decide right now?

Some days it really would be nice to not think at all—not even to wait and see. But it doesn't work. Not for long. There are people who try to threaten us into deciding. *You've got to figure out what you're going to do with your life. God will judge you. What will your friends think? Quit slacking. Make a commitment. When are you going to give me some grandchildren? When are you going to start disciplining these children? When are you going to start building your retirement? You've changed jobs three times since college; what are you going to do with your life?* [Many of these come from a parent who has a "I Still Don't Know What I Want To Be When I Grow Up" T-shirt in his closet.]

But I think it takes great courage to say, "I don't know for sure, and I'm okay. I'm going to go do my life and be open, and see what I can believe in as it comes along." It takes great courage to be willing not to know, at least not yet. It would be easier just to have it all figured out ahead of time, and it's tempting, but that wouldn't necessarily be better. There are religious people around you and me who would tell my friend Janice that she is, in fact, going to hell. But I don't blame her for having questions. She's searching. She wants to get a sense of how to respond honestly to the yearning inside her.

And let's say that you decide at some point that you're going to go find it. You're open to what the it is. You think it's out there, somewhere. I feel that way too. So you go looking, rather than wait for it to come to you.

Deep down, along with my determination not to accept someone's solution that explains everything, I'm curious. I don't want to wait forever, necessarily, although I'm not particularly worried about it. But I've been looking. We'll see.

I'm hungry. I can't define what I'm looking for, exactly, but I know it resembles a sense of place. A sense that you belong where you are, finally. It resembles love, I think. But I also know that *being in* love and experiencing the exhilaration of romance and sex, while intoxicating and good while it lasts, isn't what I'm ultimately looking for. It hasn't lasted for long so far. I've tried lots of different kinds of intoxication but surely there's something better. I'm not desperate, but the stomach in my soul is growling.

I think I'm awake. I think I see what's going on around me. And it feels to me like there's something worth trying to break into or know better. This culture feels like it's in a fitful, restless half-awake, half-asleep, half-content, half-pissed-off place. What if I wake up and meet something there, which is actually worth knowing? That would be amazing.

But, on the other hand, what if I really wake up and find that this is all there is? That would be terrible. It's tough to know whether to risk it.

Some of the places I've been looking are the stories about Jesus. I wasn't trying to become religious; I can't trust religion, and don't particularly care. But what got my attention was that the Jesus I read about was a wild, free spirit who went to parties and refused to be religious. He broke rules, touched people He wasn't supposed to, hung out with thieves and whores. I wondered if that was really true; I always thought that Jesus was the stained-glass wimp in church windows. Is it possible God is passionate and involved? Is it possible that God isn't about doctrines and regulations, but that Jesus lived a life like mine, only a few thousand years earlier? It honestly seems ridiculously impossible.

And yet, I'm finding that it is true. It's slow, but I'm starting to believe it. Janice and I have talked a lot about this. She's asked the same questions I have, and I've assured her that the Jesus I'm encountering is, in fact, an ultimate kind of human being, and that the God He talks about is worth knowing, or at least knowing a little better. Janice and I ask each other, distrustfully, "Do we have to go to church?"

I've voted that we don't have to. Going to most churches will only hurt our chances of meeting that kind of God. But there are ways to meet Him. And surely there is some church out there, somewhere, that might help. Or maybe it'd be a group of friends just talking and reading and listening together. Maybe I could use some other tool—meditation, prayer, study. I don't know, those sound pretty lame. But maybe not.

I think I know that God is up there, or down here, or in here, or somewhere. I think that I've encountered God a few times. Those experiences may or may not have occurred within the context of "church." Most of us who have "we'll see" minds have had moments in which the transcendent has brushed against us or risen up within us, but those haven't appeared anywhere near church or the Bible, at least for my friends. I suppose that it's possible for church to be where someone meets God, but it's far from automatic.

One friend of mine says that when God looks down at the Earth and sees most television evangelists, he has one of those moments like the one right before he decided to flood the world and kill everyone. I have lots of friends who don't go to church, and couldn't care less, and we just talk about life. Sometimes God is a subject in the conversation, sometimes not. It's okay either way.

I'm not looking for a fix or an answer, as much as I'm looking to know something or someone. I want to find something real. And if I find it, I don't want to turn into some sort of religious freak. And I don't want to revert to being someone in my grandparent's generation. I'm not interested in being given a lesson to memorize; I want to figure my life out. I've visited traditional churches with hymn books and organ music and a balding middle-aged man up front giving a talk with three bullet points about some biblical principle or moral issue, and I think, *Come on, God—You've got to be kidding. Surely You can do better than this.*

What I'm interested in is hearing someone's story. Not *a* story, *their* story. I don't mind listening to Bono talk about his faith; he puts it into practice and lobbies for hunger relief in Africa. And he acknowledges that he's still looking. I like to hear what Alanis Morrisette says about her time in India, learning non-Western spirituality. I think the Dalai Lama is brilliant. So was Mother Teresa. But I don't believe anything because they or any other famous person tell me to; what I want is to find something to believe in that isn't true because someone told me so, but that I can sense is true, down in my bones.

I can feel my life, like a tide running in and out past and around my legs as I'm standing in ocean water up to my waist. It doesn't seem to be going anywhere, just back and forth. But I can also feel, if I watch and pay attention, that there are tides. They move. If I just play and drift along, I'll wake up miles away from where I started. If I stand out here long enough without remembering where I am, I'll be swept out too far. I'll have missed it, whatever it is. So I tread water and keep my head high enough to breathe. We'll see. Maybe I'll pick my feet up, see if there's something worth swimming toward for a little while, and see where the tide takes me.

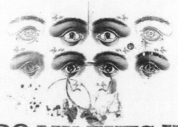

WHY DO MY EYES HURT?

CHAPTER_**2**

Rise and Shine

There is a story about a Guru who is walking down the road, and a pilgrim approaches him.

"Are you a saint?" the pilgrim asked.
"No," the Guru said.
"Are you a god?" the pilgrim asked.
"No," the Guru said.
"Well, what are you?" the pilgrim asked.
The Guru said, "I am awake."

Many of the great religious traditions say that God, in one form or another, is always speaking, always being revealed, always with us, but that human beings miss God's presence. The name "Buddha" means "The Awakened

One," and the followers of Buddha worked for years and years simply to attain the ability to see into the spiritual world. Jesus told His disciples parables, stories without simple moral lessons or solutions. He wasn't trying to keep things secret; He was just patiently revealing truths, and people would see them when they were ready to begin to journey into bigger truth than they already knew. Then Jesus would say, "The Kingdom of God—the Presence of God—is next to you. It's breathing down your neck. It's within you. If you have ears to hear, use them. If you have eyes to see, look. I'm showing it to you." A few people heard.

Wake up. Something is calling us to awaken from sleep and to leave our safe place. So how can you see this "other"? One way to learn to wake up and see what is secret is to learn how to pay attention.

There's a story from the book *The Holy Man* by Susan Trott in which people walk right by the holy man they've come to seek because they're so intent on seeing what they think is a holy man. This guy just looks like the caretaker at the monastery. They walk right by him and he ushers them through the building, shows them the rooms, and leads them out the back door, smiling and wishing them well. A few people realize he is the holy man, but only a few, because they're the ones who pay attention.

Moses walks by a thousand bushes in the desert, some of which certainly had caught fire because of drought, sun, etc. But when he finally *notices* one, it doesn't burn up. Something new has happened. The story said that when God saw that Moses had noticed, that's when God spoke to Moses and changed everybody's lives.

Growing up, I was always reading comic books and drawing the characters, especially on long trips in the car. My mother would be driving and when we were in especially beautiful stretches of landscape, she'd say, "Hey, look up. Look out that window! This is beautiful country! Hey! Pay attention!" but of course I didn't want to. I thought comic books were more interesting than mountains and sky. [A good thing about that, though, is that now I can go back and see with new eyes. Those roads are amazing now.]

Jesus' first sermon went something like this: "I have good news! God's presence is coming near! Look! Pay attention! You will be transformed!" But He also spent a long time convincing people that it would be worth the effort of awakening and seeing in new ways.

Something calls you. Danger. Suffering. Joy. Disillusionment. Suddenly, the world that was two-dimensional becomes 3-D, 5-D, 700-D. What we understand or feel becomes limitless. You know how it is when you fall in love? Suddenly you notice everything. The sky is so blue! The smell of your girlfriend's hair is so vivid. You just take it all in.

Natalie Goldberg, in her classic creativity textbook *Writing Down The Bones,* says, "When I am fully present, the world is alive." She also talks about when we let go of our everyday mind and reach out to something within us that is big, we enter what she calls "wild mind." Not tame. Not exactly safe. But awake. Able to do amazing things that don't seem possible in daily life.

The Romantic poets in the early 1800s in Europe and America talked about the alive, wild mind. The Age of Reason in the 1700s had been a time of great advances in philosophy and science, but the Romantic period was a time of deep feeling. Writers explored the non-rational, intuition, strange, mysterious. People like Whitman, Byron, and Wordsworth talked about "seeing into the life of things." The passionate, powerful Walt Whitman wrote, "I sing the body electric." Everything was alive for Whitman.

The great rock opera *Tommy* by The Who is a story of a boy who goes deaf, mute, and blind after a traumatic experience as a child; he shuts a painful world out. But then as he goes on his spiritual journey as a man, he discovers healing and sings an anthem, "I'm Free," announcing that he's regained his sensory perception—and becomes a prophet for millions of other people who also feel cut off from their lives.

The terrorist attacks of September 11, 2001, were a kind of wake-up call for many in the Western world about the resentment between East and West. Not every awakening is pleasant. Most, in fact, are not. To learn about the realities of how life really works can be horrible in how it enlarges one's perspective. But one of the good things that have come out of the September 11 experience is that many people have expanded their awareness of the many cultures of the Middle East, and learned to see what their struggles and problems are, and came to appreciate the best parts of Islam. The Old Testament is full of instructions about the importance of making sure that the Jews are the pure race and giving them permission to wipe out—physically, through bloodshed—their political enemies; the New Testament has many references to the suffering and torture that the enemies of the Christians will face. So ... we're not special here. And many people have also realized that fundamentalism and extremism are wrong— whether in Islam, Judaism, politics, or Christianity.

Ten years ago, my neighbors and their daughters went to work at an orphanage in Brazil on the Amazon River for three years. The people there live in absolute poverty unlike their family had ever imagined being in the midst of. Children were living, literally, in cardboard boxes—until the rainy seasons, when they just lived out in the open, dripping wet streets. The orphanage cared for hundreds of these children, many of whom were very ill or dying. When the young women came back to America after this experience, they talked about how they could never be content with seeing their lives contained in a suburban house, running errands and arguing over who washed the dishes last time. Their world was too big for that now.

In the creation story in the Bible, the first humans, named Adam, or "earth," and Eve, or "life-giver," are placed in a beautiful garden. God tells them they are to enjoy the garden, every part of it, except for one tree, and that they should not eat the fruit that grows on that tree. But they do it anyway. And when that happens, the story says, "Their eyes were opened and they saw that they were naked." People have talked about this as "the fall"—as in, mankind fell from relationship with a perfect God when Adam and Eve chose to eat that fruit. But it seems, too, that this experience, from a human perspective, is a story about maturing and having one's eyes opened. Adam and Eve were innocent, with closed eyes, not knowing anything about their larger nature or the complexity of human experience. They grew up. They weren't innocent anymore. They realized that life and they themselves weren't two-dimensional, that the world was much larger than the garden. Of course, they left. They had to. They couldn't live in that garden anymore. So, they go out into the world; they have children, work, and make their way. And their relationship with God doesn't stop; it just changes. In fact, the biblical perspective on the rest of human history is that it is the story of God trying to keep human beings' eyes open—open to the larger spiritual dimension within us and around us, open to God's love for us. God keeps talking to us, sending prophets and messengers and angels to us, speaking to us, and sending Jesus to us to put God and love into human terms. God wants our eyes to be open. And when we are mature, spiritually and emotionally, we want to be awake and growing in that relationship with God. Who wouldn't want that?

But ... there are a few problems.

And the Problem Is ...

A major obstacle is that we're asleep. We're limited. We're not able to hear what's being said in the spiritual realm because we live here on earth. We can't see so clearly. Our eyes are blinded by daily life: to-do-today lists, errands, money worries, and our small sense of what is real. The biblical writer Paul said, "Now I see into a dark mirror, but when I am no longer on earth, I'll see face to face." We don't see—and yet it's there, all the time.

But even though prophets and messages and dreams and signs come to tell us to wake up, most of us don't, because we don't think that message applies to us. We don't know we're asleep in the first place, like someone in a dream who thinks she's awake already. But I want to tell you something: It's not our fault.

In the old world of the middle ages in Europe, the power structure did its best to keep order. A very small group of people sat on top of the pyramid [popes, kings] who benefited from a specific cultural system, not only for their own benefit, but with a few million peasants running around, there had better be some overall sense of order, to give people and countries a way to live. So there were a few powerful, educated, rich kings and nobles, and then millions of ignorant, poor folks who did their jobs and lived sim- ple lives. This lasted about a thousand years, so it couldn't have been totally awful, though it seems so to us today. To imagine this world, think King Arthur—either the classic legends or *Monty Python and the Holy Grail*.

There was a lot of mystery and magic. Church services and the Bible were mysterious and beautiful, and in a foreign, ancient language. The nobles were a different sort of human beings than the rest of us poor, simple folk. Fairies and goblins were out there; many people never went more than a mile or two out of the village where they'd been born. The things that kept people in order were the king and his power structure and the Church and its power structure. The king could have you killed; the Church could send you to hell. So you behaved.

With the massive cultural changes in Europe that came with the Renaissance in the 1400s and after, more and more people began to think for themselves and have more access to power. Church reformations encouraged people to think about religion for themselves and read the Bible for themselves. The printing press made information available. As more merchants had access to power and money, a sort of middle class, neither poor nor rich, began to emerge. More technology and learning flattened out the power structure. The new possibilities made for changes in how people understood the world to work. A New World was even discovered.

But there was still mystery. Most everyone still believed in God and the Church, but some of the structures had changed. Why did things happen? Because God wills it. Who am I? I am simply one of God's creatures, saved by God for service on earth, and life in heaven.

Kings were losing their grip, but there had to be a way to keep the political and social structures of the cultures of Europe and America maintained. By the 1700s, thinkers came to believe that there is an order, providence, reason that holds the universe together. People studied science, poetry, the arts, and government. Its outward manifestation? Manners. If the universe is orderly, we have to behave in an orderly fashion. Think George Washington.

Mystery was starting to run and hide. No more fairy tales—that's irra-
tional. No more uncharted universe; we're charting it. Who is God? Not
the erratic, vengeful God of the Bible; God is the watchmaker, far away in
the sky, who created order, set the watch, pulled the pin, and set the universe in motion. A rational, orderly God: the Creator.

And then came the Industrial Revolution of the 1800s and more and more
dependence on machines and factories, and the creation of a few thousand
denominations and church movements, and greater and greater leisure,
and therefore the demand for more and more toys, and greater and greater
comfort, and so less and less need for God. But there was still a Church.
And many people still believed that it could send them to hell. So that
means, of course, that, since the Church had the ultimate trump card, it
was the slowest of all the institutions of the Western world to have to
change. [I think that the Church overall still hasn't really made the leap].

And so the twentieth century came. Very little mystery. Lots of leisure. Yet
also, lots of unanswerable questions. Lots of restlessness. What do those
with power do? The thing that replaced the Order of the Enlightenment
and the Age of Progress was what author and priest Richard Rohr calls a
"mass cultural hypnosis." The folks who needed things to hold together
were still—who else would it be?—the kings. But now they were called the
captains of industry. The robber barons. They created a system of capital-
ism that was about selling us stuff, stuff, and more stuff. It definitely
works—it has for over a hundred years, and it's created the most affluent
society in history. What's sad is that as we have become more and more free
from manual labor and drudgery by being culturally sophisticated and tech-
nologically advanced—which is good, believe me; I don't want to go back
to the days before toothpaste or air conditioning—but the Overall Order
of Buying More Stuff has cut us off from the natural. We don't understand

the seasons the way people a hundred years ago did. We don't see the stars. And so there's a great, deep sense of loss down inside us. Something isn't complete. Yeah, our great grandparents didn't have as much freedom as we do. But they had a connectedness to mystery and wonder that we don't. We're so rich, but we're impoverished.

My grandmother was a widow twice—my mother's father was killed as a young twenty-six-year-old farm boy soldier in Germany in World War II, and then Granny's second husband, big barrel-chested Granddaddy, died in his forties of a heart attack. So Granny never married again. But she had a boyfriend, Johnny. Johnny had a huge, multi-thousand-acre ranch outside Lampasas, this little town in central Texas in the Hill Country. It was so beautiful. We went out there and fished in the Lampasas River that ran through his place, and there was this old, rustic, natural-stone, two-story camp house that overlooked the river, built into the side of a cliff. People swam, laughed, ate barbecue and fried catfish, and played dominoes. It was heaven for me to visit when I was ten to fifteen. We rode horses and walked in the woods. I remember waking up in Johnny's little farmhouse, out on one of the screened-in porches on a summer morning. He'd be hollering at me, "Hey, boy! Wake up! Get out of that bed! There's things to do! The day's almost over!" It was like five o'clock in the morning. We'd go out to the barn and pick out the best eggs from under his chickens. We'd take some grain to the bull in the pen, check the thermometer, and get in his pickup and just go all over the place. We'd drive the tractor and disc the fields, ride horses and round up the cattle.

I know that part of the reason it was so great is that I was a kid and didn't have the worries that the adults had. I didn't have to think about house payments or rain or complicated relationships—Granny's and Johnny's was very odd, for instance, as most adult relationships are. But I am also convinced that there was a kind of order to Johnny's life that came out of his simplicity. He had one little television that picked up two fuzzy stations. He watched the weather and the news, and that was it. Television wasn't of any interest to him. He didn't worry about fashion. He didn't have existential concerns. He took care of his land—that was his environmentalism. He didn't know anything about contemporary culture—certainly nothing a teenager like me cared about. But he had wisdom. It came from sitting quietly on his porch in the evenings, watching the sun set and listening to crickets, cracking pecans open with his pliers. I know this sounds corny, but it's not. It was really true.

I am not setting up Granny's boyfriend as the noble savage or the pure, simple mountain man who isn't tainted by civilization. Johnny was just a guy. The insular nature of living in a rural part of the Southwest gave him and his culture a real fear of outsiders, and he was suspicious of and hostile toward the list he'd recite while driving down the road: "The trouble today is them wetbacks, and the God-dang Liberals—bunch of Comnist—and the nigras, and the women that want everything for theirselves." How lovely. How awful. To have a worldview that is so tiny, like a medieval peasant who has never been more than two miles away from his village. [The luxury of youth afforded that I didn't have to interact with Johnny at a philosophical level; I just enjoyed riding his horses and fishing in the river. If I were to visit him now, I think I'd have to tell him how wrong I believe he was.] So I'm not saying that his life was better than ours. I much prefer having the freedom and options and stuff that we have.

But I'm also suggesting that there is something in us that would love to be connected to the land, the seasons, the rhythms of the day, the rhythms of our own bodies. Johnny didn't listen to advertising; he wasn't interested in the latest gadget. He had enough money in the bank. He paid attention to the sky and the earth. My grandmother nearly went crazy trying to get him to buy new jeans or nicer shirts. Johnny, in his bones, was grounded. We, in many ways, are not.

What makes our lives work is technology and the drive to make more money to live—either just to make our house and car payments, which are astronomically higher than those our grandparents paid—or, if we have a little more income to spare, the drive to make more money to buy more toys. And we think we have to have this stuff. Our lives are dictated to us by the latest version of Windows. It is a mass cultural trance. We sleepwalk around, disconnected from our environment and ourselves. We get out of one box [our climate-controlled, entertainment-enhanced homes] and get in another [our climate-controlled, entertainment-enhanced cars] and go to another [our climate-controlled, entertainment-enhanced offices]. Or just stay in the box forever with our home office. We take our kids to soccer or karate. We go listen to the latest cool band at the latest cool club. We run from one achievement to another.

This capitalistic, no-rest mindset is a very real philosophical cultural system, like any other large-scaled way of life that governs how we think and live. A few hundred years from now, historians and poets will give this culture a name, just as we in hindsight have named the Renaissance and the Romantic age. I think it will be something like, The Age Of Order That Came From Being Convinced That They Would Not Be Happy Without More And Better Stuff. Okay, maybe something not as long. Maybe they'll look at how we were disconnected from anything except our own need to achieve and buy stuff, and just see us as the continuation of what T. S. Eliot called the twentieth century: The Waste Land. Or maybe they'll call this The Sleeping Age.

Poet W. S. Merwin has said that our culture is like a supermarket. In a supermarket you walk into a big room with food in it. But you don't know where the food came from. It's sealed up in metal or plastic, except for the meat—which you didn't watch being slaughtered or prepared, so you don't know anything about it, you're not connected to it and its heritage, its rhythms—and the fruits and vegetables were grown a hundred or a thousand miles away in fields you haven't seen by people you don't know. You can't smell the dirt or the rain that nurtured any of this stuff. In most cases, you don't even know what you're eating. There is all kinds of processed, unhealthy junk in these boxes of prepackaged food. A lot of it isn't food at all—it's just fake sugars and fats and seasonings and puffed something or other. Employees smile vacantly at you or stare into space like a zombie, waiting for their shift to end. There's canned food, canned music, canned culture.

On this video I have, Merwin talks to a group of kids and young adults. He holds up a leaf. He says, sounding a lot like Jesus, "With poetry, we don't just look—we see. We don't just listen—we hear." He encourages them to wake up and see the leaf, see each other. Pay attention. Feel something. He says that the function of poetry—and by implication, he means all forms of expression, such as art, music, dance, writing, drama, any work or task that comes from the heart—is to tell the truth. He says that we have to open our eyes in order to be able to do that. He then says to the interviewer that we have to awaken our senses or else we'll miss it—and he cracks up laughing on the video and says, "or else life will be like an eternal supermarket!"[3]

We are hungry for something, but the mass cultural trance keeps us wanting security and order and peace and more toys all the time. This is the most wonderful culture and day and land and progress that has ever been. Now go out and get your piece of it. The Mall Which Is America. Universal

24

[3] "Where the Soul Lives," Bill Moyers, producer, *The Power of the Word With Bill Moyers*, The Power of the Word With Bill Moyers Series, vol. 6, Films for the Humanities and Sciences, 1989.

spiritual elevator music to soothe and guide 250,000,000 people. Buy things. Don't think about it too much. That will just confuse you. Go get more stuff. You'll feel better.

No wonder young people, the ones who are still attached down deep to left-over slivers of their own childhood clarity, can feel that this isn't right somehow, and many are ticked off. It's no wonder that after the sixties when the lid blew off, music has become more and more cute, bubble-gummy, and vapid on one side, and more and more angry, caustic, and loud on the other side. Lots of modern rock and hip-hop is denigrating to women, to authority, to poverty. It's about anger. Limp Bizkit says it, on behalf of all the guy-rock hip-hop-grunge generation: *I did it all for the nook-ie*. Nine Inch Nails adds, *I wanna f—- you like an animal*.

Meanwhile, institutions such as government, schools, and churches become about being good people, and being all that you can be. God becomes a big judge in the sky who is watching to see if you behave—and also the benevolent big uncle who's there to back us up because we're the very best. Our doctrines are at heart beautiful—life, liberty, the pursuit of happiness, sharing, *e pluribus unum*. They really are great ideals. And some days we live up to them. But the system so often doesn't want to be about what we say we're about. I mean, who believes that any politician is about what the forefathers wanted to see happen? How truly reflective of what Jesus was talking about are today's churches?

Who are our warrior heroes? Sports stars. Who are our kings and queens? Movie stars. Who are our prophets and holy men and women? Pop stars. And they get caught up in it too: The pressure to be perfect and be the very, very best and have more and more and more, gives them anorexia and depression and wrecked marriages and health problems and paranoia and megalomania … just like the rest of us, only a lot faster. Michael Jackson keeps getting a new face, over and over and over. Just like we do. J Lo and all the other stars switch from one partner to another, one mate to another, over and over and over. Just like the rest of us do. Madonna switches from one look and one sound to another, over and over and over. Our Bible is *People* magazine. Our daily prayer ritual is prime time television or the weather or sports or bowing before the altar on our computer table. Our mantra is, *I must get it all done today. I must get it all done today.* The thing keeping us going is that we have bought, down deep inside, that we will be happy if we have, achieve, or become all those things.

Beauty money toys beauty money toys beauty money toys be busier be better be faster be cooler be hotter be smarter be sexier be cuter be better be busier be richer be faster be more secure be more professional be more aggressive be more sensitive be more popular be not what you already are. You are not enough. You will never be enough. So keep running. Keep running. Keep running. And at night we plop down in front of a box with pictures and sounds coming out of it, so we can stop thinking, feeling, or dreaming.

We are asleep and we don't even know it. It's as if we're living in *The Matrix* and there's a big simulated-reality software program being fed into our heads, telling us this is real life. We could wake up. If we want to know anything that's true, we have to wake up—even though the simulated reality we're in is very pleasant. Getting more stuff is really nice. It feels good. But it's like junk food; it doesn't last, it isn't nutritious, and it doesn't make you stronger. It makes you spiritually fat and lazy. We think we are awake already. But in *The Matrix*, Morpheus is trying to tell Neo that the world he thinks he lives in is a falsely constructed one—and finally has to say, "You think that's air you're breathing now?" Neo still doesn't get it, not yet. He will, but it will be difficult.

Looking at the civilized people around him genuinely baffled my surrogate grandfather, Johnny. I remember once all of us going to dinner in a really funky restaurant on the Riverwalk in San Antonio, and when he looked at the menu, he leaned over to Granny and says, "Baby, I don't want no God-dang sprouts. I want a God-dang steak." It was like taking the Clampitts out to eat in Beverly Hills. One year, I brought my portable cassette player [this was before Walkman] to his house and plugged it in and played some rock and roll on it, listening with my headphones out on the porch. He walked by after a while and watched me, with his head sort of cocked to the side, like a dog watches someone doing something odd. Then he walked off and fed some animals. That evening when I was getting into bed I started to put the headphones on again, but before I did, I noticed I heard crickets. They were getting louder and louder. Then there was an owl. And then some frogs. And then other birds. If I became still enough, I heard the wind. It was no big deal. I didn't hear a voice from heaven. But I unplugged and heard something peaceful. It was like being really awake for half an hour.

I think our culture is like that. I think that's part of what we're hungry for—some peace. You know people who've chased what our culture purposely calls "the rat race" for years and years. They can look pretty beat up. I see them all the time with crashed marriages and failed dreams and mid-life crises because all their beautiful dreams didn't come true. Of course it's sad when dreams don't come true. It's a very great thing to have so many opportunities and resources and riches. But past cultures, without so many possibilities, also didn't have all the pressure ours does to go and chase down everything and be everything. Okay, so you didn't play NFL football. Okay, so you're not a millionaire. Okay, so you don't have a washboard stomach. Okay, so you're not Halle Berry. Okay, you don't have it all together. It's no big deal. You don't have to.

We say that to ourselves, but it's only the wisest people in our culture who have figured that out and are peaceful about it. I'm certainly not. I know two people who have that wisdom. Or maybe three or four, tops. It's not easy. Those people have awakened and seen that the trance is in fact an illusion, and have decided not to participate. Like the little boy in the story of the emperor's new clothes, they have said, "Hey, doesn't anybody see that we're all pretending that something is there that isn't?"

But I'm Not Ready

Nobody likes to wake up if they weren't sleeping soundly and peacefully. And it may seem that I'm just ragging on our culture because I'm some cynic out to pop everybody's balloon. No so. There's so much about the Western world that is wonderful. There is so much goodness in many millions of people who are kind and compassionate and hard-working and simply trying to do the best they can. There is such great beauty in our culture. Such great hope. That's why I'm saying this. If we stay asleep, then the people running The Matrix get to decide what our lives are about, and the diet they've set up isn't nutritious. It's a shadow of what's really within us and outside us, out there beyond our daily grind.

We want to stay innocent. I mean, nobody wants to leave the Garden of Eden, and if you can get away with it, it's a lovely and much more comforting thing to continue to believe as a little girl in a poem by Robert Browning asserts, God's in His heaven, and all's right with the world. There's a great book by the eighteenth century French philosopher Voltaire called *Candide*, which is about an innocent young guy who wanders throughout Europe and the Americas repeating what he's been taught, "This is the best of all possible worlds"—while horrible acts of cruelty and depravity are taking place all around him all the time. But somehow he and his teacher always make sense of all the evils of culture and greed by saying, "Well, it was all for the best. God has ordained things to be this way. This is the best of all possible worlds." It's a hilarious book, even though it's painful to read, because the philosophy that we're living in Eden is just silly to anyone who, as Jesus says, "has eyes to see with, ears to hear with." We're not living in Eden, or Nirvana, or the sweet little small town in a Norman Rockwell painting. America may not be hell, but it ain't heaven neither.

So, is it not possible at all even if we work hard enough and achieve and make my dreams come true? It's nice in Eden: pleasant weather, gated community, security system, plenty to eat, plenty of clothes to pick from, seven hundred channels, servants, sprinkler system, indoor plumbing. Every product is new and improved. You gotta hand it to the advertisers of the twentieth century; they did their job very well. They succeeded in creating a new kind of human cultural identity and belief. That's huge. We actually believe that this myth is true.

I was leading a discussion a few years ago with a group of married couples in their early thirties. We read some of the Sermon on the Mount, Jesus' instructions to His followers on how to live fully, with the upside-down [actually, we're the ones who are upside-down] perspective of Jesus. It's about forgiving people who don't deserve it, using non-violence instead of weapons, giving away money without expecting to be paid back, living life in a way that points not to yourself but to God. One of the things He talks about most is the sickness of money and greed. Jesus says that we should get rid of everything we can in order to be able to focus on spiritual stuff, and He makes fun of people who think that by "building a bigger barn" they'll be secure. One woman looked at me and said, "What's wrong with building a bigger house?" She wasn't arguing; she was just genuinely thinking it through. I said, "Well, I think Jesus may be suggesting that instead of building a bigger house with lots of bigger closets, we could get rid of some of our stuff." I found out later that she was very rich and that she and her husband had just built a huge house on the lake. She wants to live in Eden and believe that it's good there. I don't blame her. Maybe if I had the money I'd do the same thing.

What am I saying? Of course I'd do the same thing. I've been running after all this stuff my whole life. Haven't you? We really do believe that American Eden exists. Maybe it's a perfect house, or a perfect family, or a perfect company, or a perfect church. There are cable television networks about each one of these ideals that show programs all day and all night about how you can have them, live in them, be happy with them. Have you noticed that there are almost no any ugly or fat or grumpy television show hosts? I wish there were some. "Hey, this is Paulie Fazzolini and you're watching *A Pretty Good House But Not One You Really Need All That Much*." It'd be a nice change. Someone on television who tells us, "You know, you really don't need all this to be happy." We say to our children that the best things in life are free—but then we also add, for everything else, there's Master Card.

In order to stop participating in this myth, you have to check out of it. You have to unplug—at least at some levels. You may have to make a big leap. And it's scary. To leave the culture that everyone else belongs to is terrifying. Have you ever seen the ones who struck out on their own and crashed? Being a rebel is fun when you're twenty, but when you're fifty, you'd better be working and making money and providing for your family, or else you're a loser. Go backpack Europe? Take some time off from your career to spend time with your family, or in spiritual retreat, or to go climb a mountain in Nepal? Okay, that's a nice vacation. But don't make it a habit.

Leaving Eden and setting out on an honest, personal, spiritual journey seems like more work than going to the gym five times a week or slaving for a paycheck for fifty years. But why is that so scary? Wouldn't it feel great to remove all those layers of what's been piled on us for years and years and years? We're growing up and all along we're being told No. No, you can't have that. No, be a good little boy. No. No. Stop that. That's ugly.

In creative writing class, one of the toughest exercises is to write without stopping for five minutes straight. Just five minutes. No big deal, right? But what happens is that you write a sentence or two and then your head says, *That's not a great sentence. I think you should rethink that one. You'd better scratch that out.* The teacher says, "You can't scratch anything out; you just have to write. No stopping. If you can't think of anything to say, just write, 'I can't think of anything to say' over and over until you think of something to say." Soon your inner censor will start panicking. *That's the stupidest thing I've ever heard. You aren't allowed to talk about that! Be quiet! Who do you think you are? That's ridiculous! Okay, okay, fine. Just go ahead and write this, and then we can always tear it up later.*

We all have this inner censor that tries to keep us from looking like total idiots. Of course, it doesn't work a lot of the time anyway. But at least it keeps things running more or less smoothly. It gives us morals and good behavior so we'll be good people and good citizens and good workers, and not make too much noise.

But if the inner censor pushes down too hard for too long, the lid comes off ... The soul doesn't like not to be listened to. In the early 1800s, English poet, printmaker, and visionary William Blake wrote:

I went to the Garden of Love,
And saw what I never had seen:
A Chapel was built in the midst,
Where I used to play on the green.

And the gates of this Chapel were shut,
And "Thou shalt not" writ over the door;
So I turned to the Garden of Love,
That so many sweet flowers bore,

And I saw it was filled with graves,
And tomb-stones where flowers should be;
And Priests in black gowns were walking their rounds,
And binding with briars my joys & desires.
[1794]

The soul gets angry if you keep it down too long. It feels like priests in black gowns are taking its dreams and winding them up in briar branches. And the soul is right; the system wants to bind our dreams with briars, or barbed wire, or surround them with land mines, or whatever it can use, so that it can feed us its dreams for us instead. The inner censor has been trained to keep watch at the gate, to keep too much freedom out. When you think about doing something or saying something too honest or rebellious, it screams, *No, don't look! I can take care of you! It's unpleasant! You won't like it! Go back inside! Nobody will like you! You'll be a freak! And your parents will be so disappointed in you! Don't dress like that! Don't make that choice! Be good! Stop it!*

Wouldn't it be great to scrape off all that stuff and be free? Just able to breathe and get into our own skin? Find out what's really going on in there?

Quit worrying so much about whether we're pleasing other people all the time? It would be amazing. Jesus announces to people, "The Kingdom of God—the Presence of God—is within you right now." Wow. To wake up and really hear that, to accept that. Something like that may be what you've been looking for, what you've been suspecting was out there somewhere.

But we can't wake up; powerful forces in us say, *No, young lady, you need to behave yourself. Don't get out of line. Straighten up.* Then, the forces say to the freedom that the Spirit offers, *Be quiet, Jesus. You make people get all excited. Get back up there in that stained glass window where you belong.*

Weird. The culture that shames us into behaving and doing the right thing all the time is the same culture that tells us that if we don't follow our dreams and climb every mountain, then we've failed. No wonder we're violent yet hopeful, health-conscious yet alcoholic, ambitious yet disillusioned. No wonder we're crazy.

In "The Emperor's New Clothes," when the emperor walks by buck naked and everyone's convinced themselves that what he's wearing is the greatest thing anyone's ever seen, you're the one who says, "Hey, that dude's naked! Check it out!" And your mom smacks you up side the head. You've embarrassed the emperor. He'll probably have your house torn down, your dad imprisoned, and your family shamed and bankrupted.

However, for anyone else who realized the truth too, you've broken the spell, you've removed the filters, you've given *them* freedom. If it happens on a large enough scale, the emperor learns to be more humble. The people become more honest and more empowered. It's a good thing.

But don't get your hopes up. That doesn't happen a lot. Jesus said that we always kill the prophets that God sends. Philosopher Bertrand Russell said in the middle of the twentieth century, "People would rather die than think." Most of the hippies in the sixties went corporate in the eighties. And, for sure, like the mom who smacks you on the head if you talk about something everybody else is trying not to talk about or acknowledge, other people in the culture will definitely resist if you do some waking up, and go on your own journey of discovery, and decide to talk about what you're learning. If a few people realize here and there that it's not a healthy thing to run the rat race all the time, it's no big deal. But what if those few people started telling other people, and then a whole lot of people decided not to accept the mass cultural trance? That's the metaphor in the movie *The Matrix*. Morpheus and Neo are waking a bunch of people up, literally, disconnecting them from the big machines that control their brains while using their bodies as sources of electricity. And so, you see, the forces that run the Matrix have to stop Neo. Lots of guns. Very exciting. Millions of people are watching *The Matrix* movies without realizing that we are the coppertops in the movie, lulled to sleep, encouraged not to think too hard, just work and support the system—even though the first movie in the series ends with Rage Against The Machine singing—shouting—"Wake UP!" They're singing to us.

The nineteenth century Expressionist painter Paul Gaugin, one of those creative people who saw the mixture of beauty and ugliness in Western culture long before the mass of people did, said, "If you make people think they are thinking, they will love you. If you really make them think, they will hate you." One friend of mine some years ago changed it to, "If you really make them think, they will *kill* you." When an entire family has decided not to talk about the fact that the dad in the family is an alcoholic, everybody helps everybody not talk about it. They develop codes [what to say or not to say and when], hand signals, and evasion tactics if things go wrong at dinner or wherever. A system like that can last for years, decades, lifetimes. It gets passed from one generation to the next. But if someone in the family wakes up and says, "Hey, that guy just threw up in the middle of the living room floor—what's that about? He's drunk or something," then the rest of you have to shut that person up, convince that person that Dad didn't just throw up in the middle of the living room floor.

And if the awakening person won't shut up, then you whisk that person out of the room, explain why we don't talk about that, and say, "That's just something that's a family secret," or give him the silent treatment to punish him. In *The Godfather*, the second-generation godfather, Michael Corleone, has his sister's husband killed for betraying the family. She confronts Michael; she screams, cries, and calls him a monster. He just had her husband strangled to death in the driveway. What's Michael's reaction? He tries to quiet her and tells her it's okay, it's not true, she'll be all right. When she refuses to shut up, he says, "She's hysterical. Call a doctor."

It's as if telling the truth about something that's scary or dangerous or difficult makes you an outcast—or crazy. There's a woman named Cassandra who makes the gods angry in the epic poem about the Trojan War, *The Iliad*. They give her a gift and a curse: *You'll be able to see the future, but when you tell people what's coming, they won't believe you.*

In the New Testament section of the Bible the prophet John the Baptist told people to turn around spiritually because God was doing an amazing new thing. It was pretty threatening to a lot of people who then turned away, but many thousands of people responded. It was good news. However, when John the Baptist confronted the king, Herod, because of something immoral the king was doing, Herod had John arrested and beheaded.

Similarly, John's disciple Jesus came and told people that God was in fact doing this new amazing thing that John talked about. It was pretty threatening to a lot of people who then turned away, but many thousands of people responded. It was good news. However, when Jesus accused the religious and social leaders of being insensitive to the poor and of abusing their power, they convinced the occupying Roman governor to have Jesus executed. "He's crazy," they said. "He's possessed by a demon."

In *The Last Temptation of Christ*, the film version of a novel exploring the human sides of Jesus, director Martin Scorcese depicted the scene where the Roman governor, Pilate, played by David Bowie, confronted Jesus. He essentially said, "I know you're not trying to lead a rebellion against us. I understand that you're no threat to the government militarily. But you are a threat. You want to change people's hearts. You want them to see beyond their lives of drudgery and obedience. And we can't have that, now, can we." So they killed him.

If people wake up and say, *Hey, why are we all running around worrying about whether our abs are flat enough? Why are we trying to get richer and richer when a mile from here there are the houses of the poorest of the poor? Is that all there is? Is that all you've got to offer? Surely there's something better to chase.* If enough people start thinking that way, the system might suffer. They won't all contribute. The machine might not have enough juice to run. So we try to convince all of the rest of us to keep playing, stay with the program. Keep your filters on. Don't start any trouble. We make fun of people who don't fit in—because we're afraid of their freedom.

The great poet Emily Dickinson wrote, in what sounds like a comment on secure religious folks:

> Safe in their Alabaster Chambers—
> Untouched by Morning
> And untouched by Noon—
> Sleep the meek members of the Resurrection —
> Rafter of satin,
> And Roof of stone....[4]

Sleep is the best thing. It's pleasant. Nobody fights too hard. Let's all just have a nice quiet evening and we'll get along just fine, okay? But then someone reads some crazy book or watches *Oprah* or discovers some new spiritual whatever, and the secure, non-threatening trance begins to be challenged. Someone asks questions. What do you do? One option is to blame the one who's asking the questions, or blame the one who won't play along or doesn't fit in. And you can always blame it on somebody else—Granny's boyfriend Johnny blamed the sixties and seventies on all the people who weren't like him: blacks, Hispanics, Jews, Catholics, women, hippies, communists, Liberals, foreigners, Yankees, the people across the street—or the son he didn't like and turned away from because the son wanted to be an actor and not a farmer, and who discovered his sexuality, and who died of AIDS. *Let's just take all them fellers and stick 'em on an island out in the Pacific and blow them suckers up. Then things will be nice and safe and we can all go back to enjoying ourselves like we did in the good old days.*

Haven't you ever heard someone say something like that? If we could just get rid of those troublemakers, things would be so much nicer. We demonize anyone who threatens us by telling the truth or even just by being different. But we especially dislike troublemakers. You know, like Joan of Arc, Martin Luther, Galileo, Abraham Lincoln, Martin Luther King, Jr., Robert Kennedy, Gandhi, John the Baptist, Jesus of Nazareth. Imprison them, assassinate them, shut them up. We enlightened people

37

say, *Oh, we would never do that today! That was different!* Yeah. Whatever.

I Get the Point. So Now What?

So who can wake up? Is it possible for anybody at *all?*

Children are already awake. That's why Jesus values children so much. Jesus said that if we refuse to be open and willing to accept what we don't understand, what we can't control, then we'll never get what He was showing people. He said, "Unless you become like a child, you'll never enter the Kingdom of God." Nineteenth century English poet William Wordsworth wrote,

> Our birth is but a sleep and a forgetting:
> The Soul that rises with us, our life's Star,
> Hath had elsewhere its setting,
> And cometh from afar:
> Not in entire forgetfulness,
> And not in utter nakedness,
> But trailing clouds of glory do we come
> From God, who is our home;
> Heaven lies about us in our infancy!
> [1807]

According to Wordsworth, we start off pure and connected to the heavens we came from. Jesus seems to agree.

So, you have it, but then the system makes you forget it. *You can't be running around talking about daisies and God and love and openness and your feelings all the time! Get to work! Start earning your keep!* So, there you go. Off to sleep now. But before children go to sleep—you know, like, in middle school—they do point the way for us regarding how to stay awake or become re-awakened. They can see things we can't, and they'll say stuff we won't. They'll ask why we don't talk about Daddy's drinking. They'll say they're tired and need to eat. Kids have to be taught to be polite and swallow their feelings; otherwise, they'll say that you have weird hairs sticking out of your nostrils. Of course, there are adults who never learn to decide which feelings to act on or not, and they're known as sociopaths. So I'm not suggesting that nobody be guided about what's appropriate and what's not. What I am suggesting is that to become like a child again is one way to awaken. Kids dance. They sing. They make art. They laugh when they're not supposed to, notice what they're not supposed to. They don't care. They're just in their own skin, and the world is still alive to them. They haven't started measuring their surroundings based solely on what those surroundings can mean to their own status or productivity.

There's a story in the Bible about an old man, Eli, who was in charge of a temple. So, he was important. Lots of responsibility. Big resume. Diplomas on the wall. He was also a terrible father—too busy achieving things.

A boy named Samuel comes to live in the temple to study to become a priest. One night Samuel is lying in bed and he hears a voice calling his name. He goes to Eli and asks him what he wanted. Eli says he didn't call him and orders him back to bed. It happens again. Eli says, "Get out of here and go to bed. I've got a lot to accomplish tomorrow." Finally Eli gets it and says, "Whoa, wait a minute—If the voice calls again, answer, 'Here I am, Lord.'" It happens. And God gives a message to Samuel, which comes true.

It turns out that God wants this boy not to become not only a priest, but also a prophet. Someone who hears God directly and speaks on what he hears. The thing that makes this kid have this amazing openness to the Spirit is that Samuel listens, especially in the darkness. Why doesn't Eli the priest hear? He is asleep, literally and spiritually.

But what if you're not a child anymore? I'm not. It's a struggle for me to really listen to my heart, or to the voice of God. It's really hard for me to put up with mystery. I need to know the answer. I need to be in control. However, I also don't want to live under the mass cultural trance. It's ultimately unsatisfying. I don't know how I know that; I just know. What's the answer? What can help me to awaken?

If you're asking those questions, you're on the road already. You're waking up. Maybe the "we'll see" mind has started to believe that there may be something to see. The life that the great myths, the great traditions, and the great paths talk about is something large. Something wild. Something you can't explain or control. It's a journey you have to travel. And its first steps are to leave the place you were and go out into a new place. As you take those first steps, you realize: *I didn't even know this was here! How long has this been here?* In the movie *Field of Dreams*, the evil brother-in-law has an awakening as he walks past the field full of resurrected baseball players and says, suddenly, "Who are they? How long has this been here? Where'd they come from?" And then he isn't evil anymore.

But the great path is not easy. I want to wake up; I really do. At least, I think I might. To walk outside after living your whole life in a dark room hurts your eyes. It's tempting to stay where you're secure. Where you already know the answer. *Pull the covers back up. Turn off that frickin' alarm clock. Let me go back to sleep.* Don't do it. There's an amazing place to go to after you start to wonder if there really is more than this. Feel those beginning stretches in the legs and arms of your soul. Swim up to the surface.

AUNTIE EM, IT'S A TWISTER

CHAPTER_**3**

So, let's say you're going to wake up, come out of a dark room, breathe some new air, and see if there really is something besides the culture you're in—but you're still resisting. Okay. That's understandable. Our entire culture is attempting not to wake up. The spiritual journey is hard. It's strange. It doesn't gel with what matters to most people, and on top of that, it's difficult at a deep level. It's about losing some control over what happens to you and how your life goes. It's perfectly natural not to want to give up control.

If you're a relatively young adult, there may not have been all that much that you needed to wake up to just yet. You're still in school, or just out on your own. Getting married. Building a family. Getting your career going. Hanging out. But even if you're not feeling any need to go through the effort of opening yourself up to some dimension of consciousness you don't even care that much about yet, your heart has been searching for a long time for something that all the stuff stacked around your daily life can't provide for you. If you already know that, then you're on the look-out. If you don't know it, that's okay. There's no hurry. When it's time, you'll know. The new thing can be happening without you even realizing the process is going on. There are no necessary prerequisites for waking up. Lots of things can cause it to happen, help it happen, whatever. Maybe you're just ready. Maybe it's time. Maybe you get hungry for it. Maybe it's working on you and you don't know it. And maybe it happens slowly—not all at once. You take small steps out of Eden. You grow. You learn a lesson, then another one, then another one. You don't ask for them, but they come, like the boyfriend/girlfriend breakup in junior high school. Junior high: the ultimate life lesson laboratory. Ugh.

The Eastern religions have a saying: When the student is ready, the teacher appears. Sometimes the teacher—an event, a lesson, a loss—just shows up. Sometimes an awakening isn't one event, but many, winding over and under each other as you walk your path in life. But at some point, it may be that the walking has brought you to a place where you can feel that something's in there, or out there, and you'd like to see it, know it—but you don't know how.

Maybe you've known people who have something they'd like to do or to be which involves large-scale change or a big personal gamble, and they talk about it for years, but they just can't make themselves go all the way and grab it? *I'd love to be a dancer, but I don't know about taking lessons with that dance teacher; she doesn't seem like a nice person. I've always dreamed of going to Africa, but the opportunity never came up. There are some people I need to forgive, but I really can't make myself do it. I'd like a new job, but the one I've got has good benefits. I don't have to decide right now.*

Our culture is about having it all. That way, you don't ever have to decide. But not deciding means that nothing happens.

Well, if you can't let go or can't see how to get there—if you're neither in nor out, but the desire won't go away—the universe may have to help you along. In fact, it already has been helping you along. It's helping you right now. You may have to be nudged just a little bit. If you can't make the leap on your own—if you can't stop waiting to see what's out there—life has to wake you up sometimes. Maybe it just happens. You don't necessarily want it to happen, but maybe you're in the right place in your life for it to happen.

In the movie *The Wizard of Oz,* Dorothy seems like a sweet, innocent little country girl. Yet, shortly into the movie, we learn that she isn't so simple after all; there is something she's dreaming about. She wants to go over the rainbow. The place where she lives isn't enough to satisfy her heart. The farm section of the movie is filmed in brown and white. No color. But the images in her dreams are in color—blue skies, lemon drops, rainbows, bluebirds.

However, in many stories of spiritual journeys, there are powerful forces that keep the young hero or heroine from being able to start on his or her adventure. For Cinderella, it's orphanhood, and poverty, and a wicked stepmother. Juan Diego of the Mexican story of Our Lady of Guadalupe isn't the right person to receive a vision from the Virgin Mary; he's a poor, illiterate Indian. David is the youngest brother left out in the fields to take care of the sheep before God picks him as the next king of Israel.

Dorothy, too, has forces that keep her at home and unable to reach her dreams. One barrier is the wicked Miss Gulch, who wants to kill her dog

Toto, the thing that she loves the most. There's also the poverty of her family. Her parents are absent. We don't know where they are, but Depression-era Kansas is a tough place to live without parents. And nobody listens to her talk about her dreams; that doesn't help either. Nevertheless, like all brave heroines, Dorothy is ready for something, and that something comes to give her a head start in finding it.

When the forces that control your life won't get out of the way and you're ready for change, sometimes it seems as if the gods send something to screw things up on your behalf. It may not feel like it's on your behalf, but it is. There's always a blessing in these things. In your case, there are probably main obstacles to your being able to get going on the next part of your life's journey. One force opposing all of us is our spiritual blindness because of our comfortable culture. Air conditioning, television, music, busyness—the soul can't break through with that much interference. In Dorothy's case, it's a tornado that picks up the house and throws it over the rainbow. You can't make a tornado appear, nor can you make it disappear. All you can do is hang on for the ride.

Dorothy's house lands and everything seems okay. She's all right. She gets up. She thinks she's still in Kansas. And then she opens that door. Spiritual journeying is all about leaving one room or house or place in your life and going out. Initiation experiences take you outside the world you live in into a larger sense of reality. And the place you go to is huge, a mystery, overwhelming, nothing you can control or even understand.

My mother talks about seeing this film in the theater when she was a little girl. When Dorothy walks out of that brown and white house, she and the people in the theater saw the bright colors and flowers and trees and Munchkins that Dorothy's seeing for the first time, and it was like nothing they'd ever experienced before. When Dorothy's journey changes so dramatically, the people in the theater were also transported into the giant leap Dorothy had just made.

Sometimes we can make it over the threshold on our own. But the great spiritual and mythic traditions say we almost always need someone or something—a ritual, a crisis, a teacher—to push or pull us over. A huge force from within us and outside us knocks on the door to our souls, then pushes the door harder against our resistance and suspicions and fears, and finally, if we keep protesting hard enough against what wants to come in—which is almost always God, God's grace—the huge thing just knocks the door down. Sometimes a tornado is required to get us over ourselves. One that has the power to throw your house around. Knock you in the head. Mess things up. Take you away from home.

Facing death can wake you up and ask what's happening. Many of the great spiritual traditions talk about death as the ultimate teacher. Sickness, too. I've talked with a lot of people who are stunned and have no way of dealing with what's happening with their lives when they or someone they love gets really sick. Your husband is in the hospital with tubes running in and out of his chest, and you're thirty-one years old. *This wasn't supposed to happen. How did life turn out like this? What is going on?* Maybe you haven't had to face too much death or sickness yet. Other things can do it. Rejection. A lost job. Disillusionment—someone you admired turns out to be a liar, crooked, weak. Divorce definitely does it. Strangely, getting everything you ever wanted can do it too. You get all the goodies and then hit the wall: *I gave up the last ten years of my life to be successful, and this is all it adds up to?* A hundred things can cause us to ask the big questions. We lose. We fail. We experience what the great poet Langston Hughes called "a dream deferred."

But this *Does Mean* Something, Right?

When something picks up your spiritual and emotional house, or knocks your door in, or takes the top of your head off, it can feel exhilarating and terrifying at the same time. A horror movie or a roller coaster does the same thing, except that you know there's a beginning and an end. In the case of something knocking in the door—walls—roof—of your life, you don't have any idea how it will end, or if it will end. You don't know anything. But we human beings have a primal need to know. So, in the panic of this moment, many times our first inclination is to try to form an answer for what just blew in. We start asking questions. How on earth did this happen, and what does it mean? The need for meaning and structure to order our lives is deep. It's where tribal religion came from in the first place, thousands of years ago, before history. First, there were the mysterious and awful forces of nature, so people dreamed families of gods who governed the skies and oceans. Soon, the gods also governed human affairs. That's just what human beings do. We want an answer or some sort of system that explains everything. The thunder rumbles all around us, and we want to run to a big parent who will tell us it's okay. In the face of the effects of a tornado—a real one or a spirit one—we instinctively want to know why what just happened, just happened. We just want to ask. That means something got our attention. That's a good sign.

But giving a simple formula as an answer for something as overwhelming as disease or death doesn't help anything; it simply keeps us from facing the fact that there are some things for which there is no answer. That's tough for twentieth century thinkers. But even in the postmodern world, in which the majority of people have let go of much of their trust in most traditional systems and institutions, we still do it. Look at all the feelings that followed the attacks on September 11. We live in a culture in which there seem to be very few universal answers, but with an event of that magnitude, we felt somehow that there had to be some answer, somewhere. Everybody wanted to explain it—politically, philosophically, or religiously. The Sunday following that Tuesday, thousands of churches were full to overflowing. Counselors' offices were overwhelmed for months. People wanted an answer.

I've been to funerals of young people or children when someone always wants to explain what's happened by reciting a nice answer that they harvested from a grocery store greeting card or Internet spam. "It's for the best." "It was just his time." "God needed another flower for His garden." "It was God's will." God the monster. *Lord Jesus, please help us,* I think to myself. People have got to stop saying this stuff. Just tell them you love them and that you're so sorry this happened. That's more than enough.

I know that for me, the idea of simply facing what I can't control or make any sense out of makes me want to run. The quicker I can get out of that spot, the better—because I'm not in control. Something in my head scrambles around, looking for an overpass to crouch under until the storm blows over, or a fortress to live in that will give me protection. In me somewhere is a desire to find some mythic, religious, political, or philosophical system to explain or eradicate the mystery of the big thing leaning against the door of the soul. Yet I also have lived enough and had enough tornados blow by that I know better. There are very few answers that can make sense of everything and tie things up in nice little ribbons. God is too mysterious to be tamed like that.

You can't be in control when a tornado comes. You can try to hide, or you can work on some mechanisms for preventing too much destruction, but ultimately, there's nothing you can do except hang on, wait for it to be over, and then see where you've landed. If the tornado knocks your house down, or the flood washes all your cattle and barns away, or disease takes away your child, or a recession wipes out your business, any control you thought you had is meaningless. You have to realign the explanations for how the world works that you, your culture, your church, or your family built.

A good friend of mine, Bill, called me up one day a few years ago about three in the afternoon and said he wanted to go shoot pool and drink beer—and he wanted to do it that night. Something was up. I said I'd come by and pick him up. So we headed to this place and got a beer and played pool. We both suck at pool, but that obviously wasn't the point. We played a while, then sat down and munched on pretzels and made small talk. Finally, he said, "I'm a good guy, right?" Sure, I said.

"I went to church. I sang in the choir. I went to college. I made pretty good grades. I got a job. I met a nice, sweet girl." I know Jenna. He's right; she's a sweet girl.

"We got married. Everything was going great. God's been good to me. My kids are great." They had two boys who were in preschool at the time.

I noticed that Bill's face turned pale as he looked at the sweaty beer coasters on the table. "I came home early Monday afternoon from work ... And Jenna was in our bed, with Michael." Michael was a friend of ours from church who worked with Bill.

Bill didn't have anything to go with here. No ideas. No backup plan. "I don't understand," he said. He stared up through the pool hall's cigarette smoke at the dark ceiling tiles. "I don't get it. How this could happen?

What did I do wrong?"

I didn't say anything. I was just there. He said, "How could she—how could they—do this to me? I want to shoot her, shoot Michael. Shoot myself." Bill is a terrific guy. He'd never shoot anybody. What he wants to shoot is the monster. The tornado.

"Why would God let this happen to me?" Now God is the monster. He looked right at me and asked, "What's the answer?"

The not-terribly-satisfactory answer to a question like that is that there is no easy answer, no formula, no explanation for why people do the crazy, painful things they do, or why we suffer, or why things don't turn out the way we want them to. A tornado just tears the house down.

Since the fragmented nature of post-sixties culture is so raw and arresting, millions of people are working very hard to deny that there was anything wrong in the first place, that with the right answers and the right formulas, all will be well. *No, no, you're mistaken; the walls of Eden are not disappearing in front of us.* Not to have a formula—even a formula that makes God into a monster—is more terrifying than the bad or amazing thing that's happened or that we've had to learn.

A very successful strategy for this camp is to deny or ignore sickness, what's ugly, or what's uncontrollable. Live in a bubble. Stay innocent. I know a thousand people who've done it. And when trouble comes, they use the simple answers that they've been taught, and that takes care of it. There are many ways to guard against having to acknowledge that the alarm clock is going off. Religion is a great opiate, Marx said. So is holding on to civil religion—*America is the greatest country in the world; America is a Christian nation. Obey the law. Be a good person. The authorities in Washington, your church, and your schools, really mean well. Be patriotic. Be a nice person.* Or you can go the other direction. You can blame it on the Devil and say that whatever we don't like is his fault. You can make any institution you don't like into the Devil—other religious groups, big business, Liberals, Conservatives, other racial groups, homosexuals, Christians, whatever. You can also choose to stay stoned so that you never hear the alarm. Addictions are seemingly great ways not to hear anything you don't want to hear. We can be addicted to a thousand things—chemicals, alcohol, tobacco, eating, playing, exercise, television, hobbies, anger, work, sex, control, indignation, victimhood, bigger toys. Anything to focus on instead of what's really going on inside us. I know a thousand people for whom this works very nicely.

The problem is, you *do* hear the clock; you just find ways to tell yourself it's not ringing, that it's someone else's alarm, that it's a dream. You're in the fortress, an arrow penetrates that fortress, and say, the arrow is on fire, and you don't know how to put it out, or it catches the hay and the walls too quickly, and the whole thing just burns down. *This can't be happening!* There's a Talking Heads song in which the character singing looks around one day and says, in shock, "This is not my beautiful house! This is not my beautiful wife! How did I get here?" And then the chorus says, "Letting the days go by, let the water hold me down." This person is in such serious denial that when his life changes, he's not even aware of what's going on, and then suddenly, he looks up in surprise, and forty years just flew by. He's lost. Denial quit working for him, finally. And when that happens, sometimes the answers don't work anymore. Your child dies and someone says, "It was just God's will." You used to believe in God, but at that moment, you've decided you don't. Some people will say it's the Devil tempting you; some will say it's a lack of faith. Maybe it's that the system you were clinging to was too small to allow for the mysteries that are bigger than we are.

If you still can't handle how big life has become, you slip into depression, get sick, commit suicide, or become destructive to others. The soul still waits. Hungry. Yearning for more than the spiritual or cultural junk food we live on. It wants something to happen. Something strong. That's why it invokes tornados. It knows something else is out there. In here.

However, despite our panicked need for an answer—any answer—if we are able to let go, those who fall into the mystery very often find that the soul can, in fact, handle it after all. Plato said, "Consider this: the soul of a human being is immortal, and therefore able to endure every sort of good, and every sort of evil." It's hard for us, in our finite, immediate-oriented lives, to accept this, but the soul can take whatever the universe dishes out. In fact, if we're stuck in our lives—as the U2 song says, "you got stuck in a moment and now you can't get out of it"—sometimes the soul *welcomes* the storm. If a part of us that's hurting or being denied keeps getting smashed further and further down into some hole somewhere—especially something we think is dark or wrong inside us—at some point, it's going to insist that we pay attention to it. In the Greek tragedies, the gods send a plague or a war to get the attention of the king or general in order to point out something that's not right but that nobody wants to talk about. All the doctrines and formulas in the world won't answer the complex issues of what's deep in the human heart. The Bible says that God is a mystery, that life is a mystery, and that trying to explain everything is like "chasing after the wind."

We can, however, if we begin to awaken, seek not to find an answer, but to simply *see* what's really going on, not judging or making sense of it. And it's possible that the soul will make it through just fine. In ancient Greek tragedies, if the hero, who is deeply flawed, is willing to face and acknowledge what he has done, there is hope. The repercussions don't go away, but there can be some healing. The city of Thebes gets healed from a plague because the evil secret that was in it—in this case, Oedipus killing his father and marrying his mother, but nobody knew about it, including Oedipus—is brought out into the open. The people of Thebes and their king had to face something they didn't want to, but life isn't made just of what we want to look at. Let's say that after finding out about Jenna, Bill decides to cover his questions and pain over with simple answers or a formula, rather than to take the journey of discovering what this experience is really about. That would mean that he gets to blame the world, blame God, blame Jenna, blame it on the Devil, even blame himself for being a horrible person—and then he can roll right back over and go back to sleep. It won't be a sound sleep, but it won't feel as horrible in the short run as he fears facing the truth will be.

If the wound is a wake-up call, however, then the person may be able to walk into a new place. If he doesn't go into complete denial, Bill might be able to discover something bigger than his own fear of not knowing the answers. And that would be a step over the threshold. That might mean a true awakening.

Bill might learn something. He might discover, for instance, that going as a happy little family to church every week isn't the same thing as listening to Jesus' urging that we serve each other and pay attention to each other's needs. He might realize that Jenna was starving emotionally because Bill was a workaholic who justified his addiction by saying, "I have to provide for my family." He might realize that his perfect wife, children, house, car, career, stereo, gun, and extramarital affairs of his own—yeah, that was part of his problem, too—weren't going to satisfy the longing in his soul.

A young man named Siddhartha was raised in a beautiful castle in India by his rich parents who didn't want him to suffer or experience anything unpleasant, in order that he'd grow up someday and become a great king. But the gods wanted something else for Siddhartha, and so one day the gods in this story revealed to him the suffering of people outside the castle, and poverty, and illness, and death. They showed him sick people, and poor people, and an old person, and a dead body. And he just flipped out. He couldn't take it.

But instead of imploding, or giving up, or retreating into religious dogma, or going into clinical depression, or committing one kind of suicide or another, Siddhartha decided to journey outside the castle and find out what's going on in the world. To find who he is, what is true. He travels a long way, spiritually and physically. He suffers. He learns a lot. And when he finally gets to the place where he can let go of all his answers, his fears, his ambitions, and his attachments, he awakens. He becomes the Buddha, the Awakened One. The world turns beautiful colors. The forces of darkness recoil in anger, but flower petals fall from the sky.

There are stories like this in every mythological and religious system. They're in the Bible as well, Adam and Eve being the prime example. Jesus, too, never promises easy answers. He promises the cross, a symbol of the spiritual deaths we have to face over and over as our answers, formulas, and the little Lego houses of our comfortable lives collapse, and we are given the opportunity to surrender to the next step in our journey with God.

Time to Die

In the book of Luke in the Bible, there's a story about an awakened man who came to be known as John Who Baptized. He was raised in one of the fanciest houses in the high-rent district of the capital city, Jerusalem. His father, Zechariah, was one of the high priests of Israel. John was a child with money, privilege, and big expectations to fill. His parents were old when he was born, and he was their only child. He was, therefore, part of the elite ruling class of Israel and its most important group, the priesthood. The control of the complex and privileged religious system was handed down from one generation to the next. And he was next. No pressure.

But something happened to wake John up. The story doesn't say what it was. Maybe when one or both of his elderly parents died, John fell apart. Maybe he saw the human, flawed side of the worship in the temple [it's in every human system] and got turned off to religion. Maybe he had an encounter with God—his father and mother had both seen angels before John was born, so it ran in the family. Maybe in this encounter with God, God told him that something was coming, and so John left his safe world to go find it. Whatever the tornado was, it sent John out into the desert, past the Jordan River. The Jordan is the boundary the Israelites crossed, 1400 years before the time of Jesus, to enter the Promised Land. They would only cross it after they walked all over the desert for a generation, getting ready for the new thing God was about to do for them. So for the Israelites, to go back out of Israel, beyond the Jordan, meant that they were leaving familiar territory and going out into a place that wasn't home. It was scary to leave the safe place. But it was also where they could find God.

We don't know who John studied with or received instruction or authority from, although there is a lot of evidence that there were communities out in the desert, full of hermits and religious ascetics. They spent their time praying and going through formalized rituals, which included bathing and cleansings, many times a day. Maybe John became part of such a religious community. That would help to explain his using water baptism as such an important symbol for his own work with people. But whatever happened, he ended up out in the desert preaching a message that he'd gotten directly from God. He'd seen or heard something, in the tradition of the prophets, and God told him to go and tell the people. The message was, "Wake up—God is about to do something important. Get ready. It's time to be changed." John lived out there in the wild, wore rough clothes, trained disciples, shouted into the sky, attacked sinners for their disobedience to God. He tells them, "You think *this* is a big step? I'm just baptizing you with water to cleanse you; the guy coming next baptizes with *fire*."

The ritual John used to symbolically cleanse people of their unworthiness to be open to the presence of God is baptism. Any number of symbolic religious acts existed then, just as they do now. But baptism is the one John chose to use. Baptism and ritual cleansing are used in many cultures and religions, and there are lots of ways to baptize someone, but they all involve water being in contact with the body. It almost always means the death of something. It's about beginnings, and endings. It's the mark of getting rid of something, having it scrubbed off, so that a new thing can shine through. Baptism is a sign of release. Of surrender. Of saying, "Alright. I give. I'm ready to go to the next thing You have for me to learn or be." One of the methods of baptism is for the baptizer to lower the one being baptized backwards into the water. It's a sign of total vulnerability, total surrender. But all methods of baptism are in one way or another signs that the one being baptized is not *achieving* anything, but instead is *receiving* a gift, and thereby moving into being a new kind of person. In *The Matrix*, when Neo is unplugged and is awakened from his sleep, he ends up falling naked into a giant pool of water. He is lifted out of that water, lying on his back, by a giant arm reaching down out of the sky. [A little while later he asks, "Why do my eyes hurt?" and he's told, "Because you've never used them." He is being born.] The act of baptism signifies that you have let go. You belong to something bigger than yourself. You're not your own anymore.

John's message was having a powerful symbolic, spiritual, and emotional effect on the people of his day. Hundreds, even thousands of people were leaving the cities and towns and traveling for miles and miles, out into the desert, making their pilgrimages to hear him speak and receive this cleansing ritual from him. They seem to have felt that if John had heard this message from God, maybe in being close to him, they could receive the message too. Maybe God would come close to them as well. Something John had experienced in his awakening was speaking to what had been cooking in the souls of the people of Israel. Israel was an occupied country, under the rule of the Roman Empire. Maybe that suffering was what was awakening them. But whatever caused it, they were ready somewhere inside to move into a new phase of their lives. Here comes a tornado.

This culture of ours doesn't have true baptism experiences—doesn't want them—moments when a part of us dies, and everyone lovingly and purposefully participates in the ritual, meaningfully. In traditional cultures this leaving home takes place in the life of a young person and often includes a ritual or literal scarring of the body—circumcision, tattooing, making cuts on the face or chest. It is painful. It is difficult. But the process is meant to show us that we are not only to realize in our heads that we're leaving home, but that we won't come out of this alive—not in the way we were before. "The former things have passed away; all things are made new" is the way one scripture says it. That sort of change requires a death, pain, struggle, and surrender. And going through this kind of change with the official sanctioning and participation of the adults in your culture makes you feel like you're getting somewhere. When you're there, you belong to the grownups. You don't have to sit at the kids' table at family reunions anymore.

But it's more than that, because it's not just the day at church every fall when children move up to the next grade in Sunday school; it involves death. We have church rituals in which kids "give their life to Jesus" and are baptized, and that's good, but none of the experiences like that that I've witnessed emphasize for those kids the part of baptism that's about dying. We talk about it, but we don't want children to experience it. All your family is there; you wear your bathing suit under a nice white robe. Afterwards everyone goes out to eat. There are rituals that take us from one place to another; we have junior high and high school, and the graduation ceremonies at the end of each. We have our first sexual experiences, but no one with wisdom helps us through those; our culture's too much in denial to talk openly about the passage of our young men and women into sexual maturity. The adults in this culture lack maturity regarding sex, so we can't impart it to anyone else. There are Scouts, or after-school clubs for pre-teen and teen groups, and there might be a sport that makes us work harder than we knew we could. But in each of these passages, we're not really required to get away and face who we really are, deep down. We don't have to die.

Parents don't give their kids up; they let them graduate, but they try to keep the kids close by, physically or emotionally. This can be especially true of the sixties children who are now parents—their job was to find it all and have it all. So they want to keep it all, even their grown kids. So we don't really have any meaningful initiation experiences in which we are moved from the safe place we've known into the scary, scarring, unknown place in order to discover ourselves through dying. And even though there are a lot of adults out there who genuinely work to help young people and love us and are helping us with our spiritual journeys, they're in the minority. We are a culture of "holding on to all things." Baptism, on the other hand, is about letting go of things.

The twentieth century was about achieving and acquiring. But that's not how the soul works. And that's maybe part of why the modern thing couldn't last forever. In many ways, the world of success and achievement and getting it all together led to the explosions of the sixties and after. Maybe that's why we're such a hungry culture, a group of people hunting for something that's missing.

When you're ready to leave one place and cross to another, it's not time to have a nice, tidy God-moment and then head back to business as usual. A quick fix of ultimate reality is no fix at all. It's like any other drug. What you really want is something real. The storm makes you ready. You surrender. You go under. Part of you dies. Then you can live.

This is seriously dangerous. It's incredibly vulnerable. It's terrifying. If you let go, you're no longer in control. You're not the center of everything. You begin to see things you don't want to see, about others, about systems you're part of, about yourself.

However, if you're a postmodern who is no longer tied to the traditions of your elders, you already know that the systems are artificial. That's the thing about the "we'll see" mind. It is strangely hopeful even in the face of its stark awareness that the structures of contemporary civilization were all invented. Somewhere deep inside, you can tell it's fake. You know all this stuff was just made up by someone, whether that was ten years ago or a thousand. It's not real. Somebody made up America. Somebody made up morality. Somebody invented the Internet, and computers before that, and television before that, and phones before that. For you, it's not that it's all marching forward—it's just marching. You get to play with the toys, but you know they're not real.

If you do sense this, it can feel as if you're just screwed. *You woke me up for this?* You feared all along that, without the toys, there's nothing else. Maybe, since everything you can see was made up and invented, what if that's all there is? You keep peeling the layers of the onion and eventually you find out that there's nothing at the center. The wizard isn't the wizard after all. He's a little bitty guy, running a laser light show from behind a curtain. He can't do anything for you. He certainly can't get you home.

Well, okay then, now that you've been jarred out of your comfortable sleeping life, and you've been thrown all over the world, and you realize there is no garden to return to, you think you'd rather stay cynical. At least the toys are something you can touch. This death and rebirth sound like a nice concept, but it isn't anything you know anything about—at least, you don't think you do. You know about pain. But you don't know about this spiritual brokenness. It sounds unnecessarily strenuous.

Wait. You know about the other things that are important and dangerous. Believing in someone or something is dangerous. Hope is dangerous. Love is dangerous. I mean real love—not just being in love, but staying with someone or something. Of course, that sort of depth and commitment isn't our best thing either. At least, it's not something culture teaches. Culture taught all the people raised before 1950 that their job was to be faithful and true. Show up. Be there. But that sort of dutiful obedience to something larger than you isn't how we live anymore. The pendulum swung a long way in the other direction. Now you question everything and pledge allegiance to what you think will work, or is already working for you—not to anything else.

But just because our culture doesn't have big answers in its central core anymore doesn't mean you don't hunger for something inside, and that you won't know it when you see it or feel it. Your house just hit the ground and you woke up. You're in Technicolor now. When you get a whiff of the real thing, your soul says, "Hey, this isn't the sitcom life. This isn't Disney. This isn't 7-11. This isn't MTV. I like all those things, but they're not it. They're all like the brown-and-white-Kansas farm. This is real. I was wondering about this."

And then you think, "How do I get more of this?" The answer you're about to discover is, some part of you will have to be tamed, harnessed, directed, and disciplined. Broken. You're thinking, "Ugh. I just got thrown this far. I don't want to go any further." But you can tell something in this is real.

Many traditions talk about the process of brokenness. The state of being broken. Jesus talks about it—cross-carrying is about being broken. About coming out of your comfortable place. And He says that people who have it all together don't want it, will avoid it.

Jesus says, "It's more likely that a camel's going to be shrunk down enough to fit through a needle's eye than for a rich person—self-satisfied, secure, unbroken, safe—to learn the great lessons and go on a real spirit-journey with God." He also says, "If you want to find your life, give it away. Carry a tool that will demand surrender, brokenness, and openness. Carry your cross." And He adds, "Just look at me. I'll show it to you. Then you follow."

Who follows Jesus when He's here on Earth? Scum. The people nobody else wants. The sick. Lepers. Women who've been suffering menstrual bleeding without stop for twelve years. The blind. The disabled. Non-religious heathens. Hookers. In other words, broken people. A centerpiece of Jesus' teaching is this: "The broken people are the ones who are going to be really blessed by God." His entire curriculum for His students is this: The real blessing, the thing you're looking for, will come if you trust something enough to allow yourself to be broken. J. Keith Miller, a spiritual guide and great writer, says in his book *Habitation of Dragons*, it must be what he calls desperate people who actually are able to get it, to wake up.

And I think that maybe everyone in one way or another is already broken. All of you went through acne, being sixteen and having the guy you love ignore you, watching your parents or teachers or pastors or bosses turn into disappointments. All of you have lost, been heartbroken, been left out, had people let us down. All of you have been told you have big feet or sunken chests or funny ears or a weird accent. Maybe everyone really is broken. Tornados have a way of breaking things. Jesus is talking to everybody.

But the ones who really get it are the ones who are broken and who realize it—the ones who have awakened, at least in some ways, or at least understand that the things they've propped their broken houses up with aren't all that stable after all. They're the desperate ones. Jesus says that He has come to heal those who need a physician. So, the question He asks people all the time is, "Do you want to be healed?" You only ask for help if you can tell you need some. A few times He just grabs people by the neck and hits them with healing, tornado style, but mostly He leaves it up to them. Some of them are desperate, broken, and ready. But He pleads with *everybody*, especially the rich, satisfied, safe ones. The ones who look like they live in American sitcom utopia. Jesus says, "I have a warning for those of you who are blessed already: You have already received your reward." Well, that stinks. Isn't the centerpiece of our culture's teaching just the opposite of Jesus'? This can't be good. The post-World War II generation before us chased individual success down as if it belonged to them personally, as if they'd each been assigned that one thing to fulfill. And here we are, a generation after the revolutions of the sixties, seventies, eighties, and nineties, and we should know better, yet we can't help ourselves. We keep chasing it, too. The Gap. The mall. Designer stuff. The fast car, or the big car, or the tiny car, or the red car. More toys. More stuff. More goodies. More muscles, a thin tummy and great abs and a firm butt. Climb the ladder. Make money. Have power. Have influence. Everyone will love you. You need to be the best. Be the best. Be the best. Be the best. Be the best. You cannot possibly slow down or take a break. It's something like a carrot being dangled by a string on a stick in front of a mule to get him to plow the field. We think that if we get all those things, we'll be blessed. But deep inside, we're wondering, Is that all you got? If I get a green yard and a nice car and Broadway show tickets, will I really be happy?

Meanwhile the soul waits. Hungry. Yearning for something more than the spiritual junk food we live on. It wants something to happen. Something strong. The great spiritual teachers all say it: "Let go. Even if it takes a tornado to pry your fingers off the cornice of the house you built, or your parents built, or your grandparents built. Let go." We don't want to let go voluntarily. Jesus encourages us to, but we don't want to.

It's no fun. It goes right by us. That's natural. Every person is the same ... or else why would the great teachers have to keep telling us this stuff? The recurring message is: Be broken. Let go. Stop. Just stop.

God is wishing you the very best thing. God doesn't want you to suffer, but

God won't stop it. If it takes a tornado, God didn't necessarily send it, but God's not going to snatch you out of it, either. Maybe you need to do some flying. Maybe a little butt-kickin' wouldn't be so bad for you. Whatever gets you moving.

Those of you with little children know how you want to protect them from everything—don't let them fall, don't let them get hurt. After a while, if you are wise, you'll realize that a little pain and struggle are okay, even beneficial, for your kids. You'll do everything in your power to keep your child from harm—but for them to get hurt here and there, and then to learn from it, is to grow up. And that goes for grownups too.

God wants you to see and experience what is broken—that's what those initiation scars are about. Not to harm you, but to make you pay attention to and see where the brokenness already is. You're already broken, deep down, all over. Our culture wants you to sleep through it and not feel it. God doesn't wish you pain, but God is willing to let you do some learning.

And there is a place in your life when you will be ready to step over and see something new. Something you didn't even know was there, or that you didn't think you were missing.

The Bible says that after He comes back from being dead for two days, Jesus appears to a number of people. In this new, odd, amazing, not-like-his-old-one body, Jesus is hard to recognize at first. They knew Jesus, and they thought they knew all about him, but they didn't know this eternal part of Him had been there all along—and now it was set free and could shine.

You jog further than you ever have before and amaze yourself with joy. You say something to your children that you swore you'd never say because it's what your father always said to you, and surprise yourself with sadness. You commit a small or large crime and you didn't know was inside you, but there it is, confronting you. You fall in love, or have a child, and your sense of what love was gets blown a thousand times bigger than you thought was possible. Amazing. You forgive someone you thought couldn't be forgiven. There it is again. These moments mean that you are on the road that tornados of various sizes have been rolling through.

One of the people who responded to the call of John Who Baptized was a young man named God-Saves, a common name at the time, which translated is "Jesus." He comes through the crowd and tells this spiritual guide that He wants to be baptized, to undergo this ritual along with all these other thousands of people.

We don't know why. We don't know what caused Jesus to have His spiritual awakening. The biblical accounts don't say. They don't talk about His young adulthood. All they say is that He shows up, standing there in front of John. But something must have happened. When the texts talk about His work as an adult, they mention His mother but not His father; scholars assume that His father has died. Maybe His father's death freaked him out. Maybe some other tornado got His attention. It might've been something beautiful; He was definitely one of those people who are just gifted—and burdened—with the ability to hear from God. Somehow, Jesus' filters had been removed—or were never there in the same way that other human beings have them. But whatever it was, Jesus was ready. Jesus had had a personal awakening, and He was now ready to cross a threshold. He was ready to die and be reborn.

One of the things Jesus would teach in His school was that new things can't come without death. "If you're determined to hold on to your life no matter what, it's going to disappear, but if you want to be able to hold on to your life, quit grasping at it and be willing to lose it … unless you put a grain of wheat into the dirt, and it seems to have died and been buried, it can't grow up and become a plant that can feed people." He got it. He understood about leaving the brown-and-white room and walking into the Technicolor kingdom of being awake.

He had listened as the clouds rumbled over His little village. He had walked out to see what it meant. And what it meant was that a new thing was about to happen. He had felt it in His heart. So when His heart was ready, He traveled out to the desert to be baptized, and die, and find out what would happen next.

For your sake, and I mean this—and I sincerely mean it in a loving way—I hope a tornado of one kind or another, large or small, will come and kick you around. I've had it done to me, and maybe you've had it done to you. It stings like crazy but then you become stronger. So let's have some more. *Continue to wake me up, God.* I don't like it. It doesn't usually feel good. But it is good to be on the journey out of the old, small places and into the new, open, airy, dangerous, wonderful places.

The greatest blessing doesn't come from staying innocent. The greatest blessing is outside Eden. The greatest blessing is in growing up, in realizing that your journey can lead you to know God, but now it won't be a God that you take for granted, it won't be anyone else's ideas about God. This will be yours.

There is another step, and you're longing for it, way down, even though you don't know it, don't know how to define it, don't know what it is. You're willing to go through baptism—the letting go, surrendering. You are ready to find a deeper meaning in your little life. You say, "Okay, send me to the next thing"—whether you mean it deep down, or you're simply doing it because you can feel it's the right thing to do even though you don't understand it. If you're on a healthy spiritual journey, there is a next thing. After you take the plunge, you come up and realize that you won't be the same anymore. But it doesn't stop there. There's some more. Keep going.

WELCOME TO THE DESERT

CHAPTER_**4**

"And the Spirit of God drove Jesus, sending him into the empty places." —Mark, chapter 1

You begin to awaken, even though it hurts your eyes. Then the tornado comes and throws you around a while. You realize something needs to happen. You lose a lot of your illusions. You realize maybe you weren't so safe after all. Things aren't so secure. And that frees us to get on with it. It's time to live, to graduate, to get liberated.

So you say, "Okay, I'm ready. What do I do now? I'm excited!" In *The Empire Strikes Back*, after Luke Skywalker begins to see the larger spiritual world and is ready to dive headlong into it and go save the universe, he says to his master Yoda, "I'm not afraid!" Yoda, knowing the trials that are coming, says, "You will be … you will be." When I first saw that movie as a teenager, I didn't get it. Why would Luke need to be afraid? Why can't he go save everyone? But I think I know better now, twenty-something years later, having had life kick my butt a few hundred times.

As the water flows over Him in His baptism experience, Jesus has His personal awakening, His moment of enlightenment. He is seeing the world beyond, the world that glows within everything. In that moment, the text says Jesus has a vision of "the heavens being ripped open" as a dove descends on Him, signifying that God's Spirit had entered Jesus. The image of an animal appearing and identifying with a person in a transition in His life is reminiscent of many mythic traditions, including the Native American pattern of a spirit-animal that the initiated one sees on a spiritual journey. Furthermore, the fact that in this story, the Spirit is in the form of a dove suggests that this is a moment of beginnings and of God's promises. In the Old Testament story of Noah and the ark, the dove is the bird sent out from Noah once the rains have begun to recede, and comes back to signal to Noah that all will be well. Jesus hears God say, "You are my chosen son, whom I love." This is an ultimate, amazing, life-changing moment. In a few months He'll go back up to Galilee, where He's from, but He won't move back in with His family. He's grown up now. He's left. He has to do something else.

So, we assume when we read the story, He's ready. God just said so! Now He can go and gather His group of disciples, begin His life's work, build a great career, make His mama proud. *I've graduated. I made the honor roll! Time for me to go be successful.* But, in fact, Jesus is still not ready to begin His life's work. The modern world is all about knowing the right answer, having the right resume. However, like the ancient world, the postmodern world is much more about not knowing—so that you can know the larger thing, the mysterious thing. It is out there. And it is inside you. And that means you have to go deeper than something you can objectify or know only in your head.

You ask, "Wait. Wasn't I already in the desert? Didn't a tornado come and throw my house across the face of the earth? Haven't I gone through an awakening? That was pretty hard already. I've done some surrendering. I've gone through some emotional baptisms of one kind or another. I'm willing—and that took a big leap. None of my friends understand the questions I'm starting to ask. Wasn't Jesus already in the desert, studying with John? Didn't He already leave home? Hasn't He already been out there, giving up His security as He searched for the next thing that would happen in His life?"

Yes. He went to school out there, learned deep lessons from the prophet. Yeah, He's gone a long way already, just as you have. And when He was ready, He had a direct spiritual encounter, a vision of God, and saw the heavens ripped open. But the gospels make it clear that it's not until the moment of His baptism that Jesus is ready even to begin moving into the spiritual and personal depth and commitment that would be the center of His work. According to Luke's account, Jesus had a sense of it when He was a young man and began studying the Scriptures, and yet that at this moment, Jesus' baptism is the true beginning of His growing up. But to continue that process, Jesus has to go all the way. And that will only happen in the desert—not as part of John's school, but on His own. He has to go face His Enemy.

And when you go to the desert, you go alone.

Jack goes up the beanstalk alone. Adam and Eve leave the garden and think they're alone, although God is watching them all along, taking care of them. Moses has to go up the mountain alone to meet God. Native American men take their young males and leave them in the wilderness, instructing them not to return until they've seen a vision. Every young hero or heroine must go on some sort of search out into the uncivilized places, alone, except perhaps for a horse or a servant. Sometimes it's to fight dragons; sometimes it's to find something that is lost. But the real thing they are sent to seek is a part of themselves that can't be known until they get out of their safe environments. Away from their parents, tribe, community, or family. Away from their childhood. Away from their innocence. And it's always about returning home someday with the greater knowledge within of what is true.

The story says that the Spirit guiding Jesus—the Spirit that God has just sent to Him in the form of a dove—sends Him on a journey. It's common in traditional or mythic stories for the hero, once he's had an ecstatic or mystic experience, to be tested or tempted immediately, in order to see what he's made of. Reality sets in. You fall in love and then you realize to your horror that he's really an idiot. You come down from the mountaintop and have to contend with jerks. You win the lottery or strike it rich or get famous or whatever and then you realize you're still a human being; you still have to live in the real world. And when you look at the people around you, whether they are familiar or famous, you can see whose souls endured this testing, and those who weren't willing to stop long enough to find out what they could handle and what they couldn't: lottery winners who spend all the money they'll ever get in six months; movie stars or athletes who crash and burn, whose marriages disintegrate, or who fall into drugs or alcohol; twenty-six-year-old computer executives or lawyers who become crazily wealthy in a year or less, and then waste their lives on sports cars and stupid living that leaves them emotionally bankrupt. They didn't make it. As Jesus puts it, they gained the whole world but lost their souls. I'm not talking in religious terms; the issue here is more than religion. This is just who you wake up with every morning, staring back at you in the mirror.

So it's obvious that this testing is necessary. You rationalize it and say that it's a necessary evil, but not something to be encouraged. But the disappointing thing, for those of you who would like for everything to go your way, is that the Spirit of God leads Jesus into this temptation experience. It's not that the Enemy—evil, the Devil, whatever you want to call it—tricks Jesus into it. This is something that God wants to happen. The original Greek text can be translated that the Spirit drives Jesus into the wilderness in the way that someone drives animals, whipping them and forcing them to pull a wagon or go into the correct stall. Yes, that sweet little dove has a big stick and is beating Jesus' soul with it. And to ignore this story by reducing it to a theory about what temptation means is to miss how difficult this was, how much it's like your story and mine. Jesus doesn't want to do this. It may not even be what He expected. Maybe He thought, *Hey, now I've seen God and have experienced God speaking directly to me in a way that God never has before. I am the beloved. I am ready. Time to go start my ministry.*

As soon as I graduated from college and got married and got a job, I thought, "Man, this is it. I am ready. I'm a grown-up now." And in some ways, I was. But I wasn't "there" yet. I'm still not "there." My struggles along the journey have helped me be less about myself and more about something larger than my own agenda. I'm not as ambitious as I used to be. I'm more still than I used to be. That comes from having to figure out not just what you want, but what you can handle and what you can't. And that's not a punishment; that's a gift. Seen in human terms, Jesus is a brilliant young adult, ready to go out and get on with His life. And God wants Jesus to do that. So God gives Him a gift. God says, "You're my beloved son. I want the very best for you. Now go struggle a while." How Jesus responds to this season in the desert sets the tone for everything that comes after it. This is life and death stuff. This determines what His life means.

Jesus is in the wilderness forty days. In all religious literature or mythological traditions certain symbols are shorthand for something larger. Monsters, dragons, witches, storms—these all represent the forces outside us and within us that terrify us because we can't tame them. The journeys aren't necessarily about physically traveling from one location to another, although the places where they happen are usually real; the journey is about something that happens in the soul. The symbolic number in the Bible for cleansing through purification is forty. In the story of Noah and the Ark, God purifies the earth from evil by making it rain for forty days and forty nights. When the Israelites leave slavery in Egypt, they don't have faith that God will let them enter the Promised Land safely, so they have to wander around in the desert forty years until they're ready. For many religious people, the numbers in the Bible are literal as well as having larger meaning, so Jesus' time in the desert may have actually been forty days long. For others, it may mean a time in Jesus' life in which He was struggling with His calling from God. Either interpretation is fine with me. The point is, this season—however long—in Jesus' life was a time in which there were some things that had to be gotten rid of, or purified and focused, so that He could become stronger and more purposeful. He understands that he had to get rid of that anything that wouldn't help Him accomplish what He felt He'd been called to do.

One spiritual exercise that can get your attention is fasting. Jesus fasts—goes without food—for forty days. To go without food is a way for you to stop thinking about other things. For a long time all you can think about is food. If you've had your own dieting experiments, you know that all you can think about for a long time is the foods that are prohibited on your diet. In Jesus' case, He just had His baptism. He saw God. And then He started being denied the basic stuff He used every single day. Food. Shelter. Water. Whatever is fundamental. I've heard religious teachers suggest specific fasts that aren't about going without food—for instance, a fast from all media for a day or a week, or from the computer, or from sexual activity for a certain time, or from being around other people. All of these aren't about themselves; they're about getting your attention. Focus. Paying attention to where you really, really are. If you can keep eating or watching television or talking to people, you don't ever have to deal with who and where you really are. You can just stay busy. That comes from our need to control everything, which comes from fear.

Postmoderns are the worst about this. Worse than our I-want-it-all parents and our I-will-be-dutiful grandparents. They crammed their heads and bellies with the fat of the land and the instant culture that emerged after World War II, even as many of them also hoped that there was some meaning out there to be found. However, most people under thirty-five today don't see much hope in anything out there, but instead of going into the desert of spiritual searching, we just sit around and eat. We consume. We can't help ourselves. We eat junk food, watch television for hours on end, play sports, play video games, play computer games, watch DVDs and movies. We consume fitness, exercise, diet, running, yoga. We drink. We smoke—cigarettes are very much back in. The idealists of the seventies stopped smoking because it was bad for you. Now you say, "Screw it; who cares? I won't live forever and what's worth living that long for anyway? This place is a total mess. So I'll just have another Happy Meal, another cigarette, another sexual encounter."

But when you go into the desert—when your life demands that you go into the desert, when a tornado comes and throws you into it, since you're probably not going to go voluntarily—you are deprived of all those consumables. It's just you and your own stuff. You are made to pay attention and see what's really there. And it hurts. It isn't fun. You get thirsty and hungry. You get tired. You forget what time it is. You get lost. You get scared. You get angry. You don't get to take your weapons. All your achievements, all your goodness, all your power in the world. All your control. When you're busted, they take away all your weapons and just put you in the cell with the other convicts. You're not special anymore—which is, of course, the ultimate punishment in a consumer culture.

In modern terms, you can avoid this problem. You can think of this as a testing process—like a product assessment. You get a new toy, or you build a new invention, or you get a new job, and then you test it out, or put it through a series of steps, to decide if you want it or not. You're the subject; everything and everyone else is an object. You get to decide. How American that is—life, liberty, and the pursuit of happiness is about everything and everyone else making me happy.

But when truly spiritual journeying into the desert, you're not the thing deciding. You're part of a cosmic struggle larger than your own mood or decisions. As in an initiation experience, you want to be in control. This tendency is very human. And very American. And very modern. We're such individualists. We feel this pressure all of our lives to go out there and prove ourselves, achieve, make sure that we measure up. That's what we think matters. But Jesus' temptation isn't about how strong He is. It's about what He trusts. If you trust something, you'll let go. If you're afraid, you keep grasping at everything. But this is a part of your journey that is about not grasping. It's about learning what you want to grasp, and seeing how far you can be pushed before you either grab it again or realize that that wasn't what you wanted after all.

Twelve-step teachings say the toughest thing to do is to tell the truth. Just to tell the truth. You're afraid to face who you really are because it's just too scary to admit that you don't have it all together, that you really are afraid, that you lie or cheat or covet. You don't want to go "digging in the dirt" as Peter Gabriel sings on his CD, *Us*. You'll find ugly, hidden stuff down there that should've stayed buried: the stuff you're scared to admit is a part of yourself, the stuff that you are willing to look at, but only symbolically and only in a controlled experience such as in a horror movie. But the crazed slasher isn't out there; he's within. That's why he has to die at the end ... though there's always that hint that you can never really get away from him, that he still lurks out there, that there'll always be another sequel.

One of the most significant villains of the last generation is Hannibal Lecter. He is brilliant and outsmarts everyone—so that makes him very dangerous—and his most horrible symbolic characteristic is that he might try to eat us, like the witch out in the forest who's going to eat Hansel and Gretel or the wolf in grandma's clothes in Little Red Riding Hood. The differences between our culture and the culture that produced those fairy tales are obvious: The witch and the wolf are killed at the end of their stories, but Hannibal Lecter lives on. It's also significant that he is allowed by our storytellers—therefore, that means, by us—to kill the people we don't like. So in a weird way, he's a part of us that we'd like to let out only when we want him—but you can't ultimately control him. That sense of uncertainty reflects the postmodern "we'll see" mind. We're not sure there'll ever be a definitive answer, or that you'll ever wipe out what is angry and unmanageable. The reason the house is haunted in many horror movies is because they built it over a cemetery. The ghosts are always out there, lurking.

The things that you know are in there but which you've been told to suppress—that's the villain; that's the monster. When you're growing up you hear your parents, other kids, and your teachers telling you, "No. No, don't make that face. No, don't draw on the walls. No, don't eat with your mouth open. No, don't pick your nose." And then the thing you carry with you isn't just a "no" about your habits; it's a "no" about yourself. *No, you didn't please me. You didn't measure up to our expectations. You're not good enough. You've been a bad little girl. You're not getting a promotion.*

After a while, you begin to believe it. These things people say build little houses somewhere in our hearts, and plant little grassy lawns and buy table lamps and beds. They stay. And stay. And stay. Eventually, you don't realize that you've accepted that they belong inside you. You accept that the monster is you, or at least a part of you.

So you go into the desert and, as it turns out, you're not alone after all. All those voices and all those fears and all those doubts came with you. Not all of them are bad; you also brought with you the things that you can trust, that came from the people who believe in you. You brought the memories of days with your grandparents, or that first big project you felt so great about finishing. You bring your own sense of what is important. You bring the things that were said to you in love by your teachers or friends or parents. You bring everything.

What happens in the desert, then, is that you continue the waking up process by confronting and facing your filters, the things that are telling you who you are and what your life is about. You see them. You realize what's good and what's not so good. And one by one—or all in a bunch—the things that are surface layers of who you are, are stripped away. The filters are removed. Maybe it takes a week. Maybe it takes years.

You fight this. You don't want this. The screens and layers of stuff that you've got took years to accumulate and construct. *I can't let all that go!* You say. *That's my stuff!* What's really scary is that sometimes even the good stuff has to go too. All of it. Everything. It's time to get naked. Time to see what you've been hiding all this time. Fear comes out, maybe quietly, and maybe not. The desert is a time in which you face the villain, alone—because you are the villain as well as the hero. You face what you brought into the desert. You face your own tendencies toward what you're afraid to let go of. And in that process, your nice clothes are shredded, your hairdo messes up, and your makeup runs off. Nobody cares about your status—there's nobody there to care. You are naked, even if you've managed to keep some clothes on. No one is there to read your resume. It doesn't matter what a good person you've always been, just as it doesn't matter what a bad person you've always been. No one is there to reject you or approve of you. Which, of course, is part of why it's so awful.

And, too, it scares us because we don't have any practice at it. In our culture, it's as if we never stop being kids. A number of observers of our culture have suggested that adolescence lasts from twelve till about thirty-five. In other words, as long as you're still playing or keeping your options open—"I still haven't decided what I want to be when I grow up"—you're not grown up.

I know, I know, growing up is overrated. It's spiritually healthy to stay childlike, right? Not to be so serious all the time. Even Jesus said that we are to become like little children if we want to enter the Kingdom. But it's one thing to resist the modern world's demands to get to work and lose your soul. Yeah, resist that. Definitely. Don't give in to the burden of being part of the system. The system kills the soul.

But so does never growing up. The modern culture doesn't understand much about soul work. So of course we want to avoid adulthood. Adulthood in the modern world had a tendency to kill the soul, although our grandparents' souls were often satisfied to be loyal and hardworking because they believed in the larger pattern of the culture they were part of. But for us postmoderns, who don't trust institutions and therefore can't put ourselves on the line to serve the system for fifty years, there's not a lot there. Post 1960s culture is split. One side says, "Go to school, get a job, be a good person, and live a good life. Grow up." The other side says, "Stay young forever. You don't have to commit to anything." Mick Jagger—the ultimate Peter Pan, dancing around at sixty, fathering children and leaving wives, makes millions of dollars while staying a little boy. Don't get me wrong, I love the Stones and rock and roll. But rock and roll is in many ways a symbolic reaction against the modern demand for obedience to a repressive culture.

True adulthood, true accepting of one's calling in life, isn't repressive; it's freedom. Jesus says, "If you want to find your life, then get rid of it. Pick up your cross and follow me. I'm headed to death—but that will lead to a dimension of living that you can't imagine. You won't believe how beautiful it will be if you find something worth living for." That's what it is to really grow up. That's not restricted to being a good person. Being a good person won't help that process at all. What Jesus is talking about involves being willing not to be successful or beautiful. Truly letting go. That doesn't mean selling out and getting a job and having no life; it means finding a reason to live that is larger than you are. But you don't just sign up for it somewhere. Finding truth is a painful process that requires deep searching and lots of surrender. It means going deeper into the desert. That kind of growing up is about freedom, all about venturing out, not about giving in.

Jesus' followers saw Him as the embodiment of God here on earth. But they also saw Him as a man. I think Christianity doesn't get that most of the time; Jesus is a mythological figure, or something symbolic, or a theological concept. But the early Christians insisted that Jesus, even with the objection of their Greek philosophical culture, was both the image of God, and fully a human being. They explained this by saying that God was incarnate in Jesus—literally, that God became meat. Jesus was a fleshy, sweaty human being, with struggles like ours. And, like any other human being, Jesus had to find out what He was going to live for. He had to find a way to be part of something larger than a human being's agenda, fears, and comfort.

He came to the school of John Who Baptized. He may have stayed a while and studied. We don't know. We really don't know for sure anything about Jesus' background, what He studied, what or whom He knew, except that we know He was poor. Maybe that's what prepared Him for His spiritual awakening. Maybe He was, in a way, desperate. As I mentioned earlier, Jesus decided to undergo baptism. And when He comes up out of the water, He has a vision of the supernatural. He sees the heavens ripped open. He hears God's voice. The Spirit of God flows down on Him, flutters down like a dove. And immediately, that Spirit pushes Him out into the desert.

The traditional word for this experience has been that He was "tempted" out there by the Devil. But translators often say that a better word in modern English is "tested." He was given a test. I had this teacher in high school who used to smile as she was giving us our tests and say, "I don't want you to think of this as a punishment. I want you to think of this as an opportunity. A test is a way to see what you're made of." We'd be in the back of the room thinking, *Crap, I don't want you to see what I'm made of.* And that's often true of human beings. There is a part of you that doesn't want to be tested or measured. It's a lot of work to get ready for an assessment. And it makes you vulnerable. It makes you feel weird and unsafe. *If I don't put myself out there, then I can't get hurt too badly.* And, like Kat in 10 *Things I Hate About You*, if you're never vulnerable, then you get to judge everybody else and still keep everyone else's judgments of you at a distance.

There is also within you, though, a compelling desire to be tested in some way for which you can prepare. If it's something that's in your heart, something you want to do or something you believe in, you want to rise to a challenge. You run every morning, even when you don't want to, and then in six months, run a 5K race or maybe even a marathon. Or you work really hard on a project at your office, and when it comes time to do your presentation, you're ready. You write a book, and then you want people to read it and talk to you about it. You study for a spelling test—and then, if the teacher shows up on Friday and says she doesn't want to give it after all, you get mad. *Hey—I studied for that test! Give it to me!*

I wonder if Jesus had studied for His test in the desert. I think He had, although I don't know how He'd study for that sort of test. You can't cram for a struggle in which you face your deepest fears and ambitions. You just have to do it. And yet, you're always being tested, every day.

Every day we are preparing for the next test. The great twentieth-century British teacher and writer C. S. Lewis said in *Mere Christianity* that we human beings eventually end up turning into whatever it is we are trying to be or pretending to be all along. Maybe that's part of what happens when we are in the desert: We find out what we're pretending to be, and whether that's really what we want to become.

The story calls the thing that Jesus faces "the Devil" or "the Enemy." I don't want to get too far into the issue of how to interpret what the Bible means by that word, but scholars are pretty clear that it's not a mythic little guy in a red suit with horns and a tail. The tradition of many Christian theologies is that the Devil represents what is evil or anything opposed to what God wishes for. Over the centuries that idea—like every other concept in the Bible — evolved. [Nothing in the Bible is very simple. If the Bible tends not to make sense, or if you've never read it, you're not alone. It's an odd book.] The ancient Israelite book of Job pictures a royal courtroom in the heavens in which God is the magistrate who sends out someone called Hasatan, "the accuser," a sort of district attorney going around over the earth, pointing out wrongdoing or areas of concern. This is not only found in the Bible; in the Greek tradition there are the Furies who fill that same function, and similar characters are in other traditions.

In the New Testament section of the Bible, the part that tells the stories of the Christians, Jesus talks about Satan, a spiritual being and an enemy of what Jesus is trying to do. When Jesus' disciples do amazing things because of their trust in the Spirit of God, Jesus says, "I saw Satan fall like lightning from heaven," though Jesus never really teaches anything about what Satan is or what he's doing in heaven or elsewhere. But one of the ways Jesus demonstrates the power that God's love has to make people whole—what the Bible calls "salvation," or wholeness—is to send away embodiments of evil, which the gospels call "devils" or "demons." Christian theologians have explored for centuries all sorts of interpretations of what Satan or The Devil or Lucifer means spiritually, but the Devil is generally seen as the one who represents all that attempts to keep the love of God from healing the world.

The Christian tradition has attempted in a thousand ways to explain what went wrong with people—their fears, meanness, pettiness, brokenness.

The Bible uses the word "sin" to express something within us, our tendency towards self-destructiveness that leads us away from being complete, healthy human beings. We're not whole. We're stuck somewhere. It's deep inside us, and we feel powerless, in many ways, to do anything about it. Is it a force outside us that tries to influence us to do what is against God? Is it a sort of collective evil that is part of what the Bible calls "sin," that is, the broken and fearful condition of human beings? Is it something within us, our tendency towards self-destructiveness that leads us away from our own health and wholeness—what the Bible calls "salvation"? Whether your particular faith system, if you have one, believes that there is a literal devil, or you don't believe in evil at all, think of the struggle in the desert this way: Jesus goes into the desert to wrestle with what He believes is going to attempt to keep Him from achieving His work. Anything that keeps Him from becoming what God is calling Him to be is His enemy.

A century ago, in exploring the complexities of the human person, the groundbreaking psychologist Carl Jung talked about the Shadow. Jung's explanation of the war within was to say that you are at odds with your own Shadow self. The Shadow is that part of yourself that you don't want to acknowledge, which society or morality or guilt has forced you to shove down or back out into the darkness. The Shadow is your not-permitted self. Sometimes you refuse to acknowledge the Shadow is there—even though the soul knows it's there, and the soul longs for the Shadow to be dealt with. In some traditions, people make the Shadow their enemy and fight it, as if it were external, rather than an internal, force—a devil that is trying to attack and harm. There's no doubt that the New Testament writers characterized Jesus as recognizing much of what is wrong with human beings as being that kind of evil. And in their telling of Jesus' testing in the desert, the Gospel writers see the forces that Jesus is struggling with as the enemies of what God is trying to accomplish through what Jesus is doing.

But even in the Bible, this issue isn't simple. According to writer and teacher Richard Rohr, Jesus never teaches that the Shadow is the problem. He doesn't point out people's evil sides, or make them feel guilty, or tell them how sinful they are. He does the opposite. He acknowledges that people have "sin" in their lives, a destructive force that harms them and other people. But He doesn't pay much attention to people's "sins"—that is, the list of all the things they've done wrong. When He perceives that someone is being attacked by what the stories call a devil or demon, Jesus tells the thing to leave that person alone, to "come out of him." When that happens, the person is whole again. Jesus doesn't say that the person is bad; He says that the thing that is broken within that person is bad.

So, the people who are battling their demons or Shadows aren't the ones who make Jesus angry; rather, Jesus is angry with the people who don't acknowledge that they also have that same battle. Rich people who are satisfied and happy make Jesus sad and frustrated. Religious people who see their own separation from "sinners" make Him furious. He says they're the ones who are really the sickest. He throws furniture at them. He calls them devils. To refuse to admit that you have anything to struggle with is evil.

To struggle is not evil. To be in combat with what makes you sick or broken does not make someone a devil. Gospel stories demonstrate that because Jesus is so open to God's power, whenever Jesus is around, whatever opposes Him simply runs and hides. Screams in terror.

How did Jesus get this power? How did He figure out how to vanquish and silence devils? How did He learn how to heal those who are fighting with their Shadows? Jesus had fought with His own Enemy. Jesus had been to the desert. He had looked deep at the things that could keep Him from being who He needed to be.

Satan asks Jesus three things about Himself in the desert. In human terms, this test is not told in order to establish a theory about God or about Satan. The test is not theoretical, not about the nature of sin or any other theological issue. The test is a real process through which a real person traveled, just as you and I do. Whatever Jesus would choose would determine the course of the rest of his life, just as what C. S. Lewis's observation about our tendency to become what we keep working on being asserts about all of us. To set the stage for how Jesus' Enemy will be able to attack, the story says, first, "and Jesus was hungry." He is in a deeply human place here. He's struggling. He's vulnerable. In a sense, Jesus is struggling in the desert not only with an external Enemy, the symbol for what opposes the purposes of God, but also with Jesus' own Shadow.

The scriptures say that Jesus was a human being in every way—except that the brokenness of other human beings wasn't present in Him. He was "without sin." The scriptures also say that Jesus learned this, through obedience to God. Jesus is here learning obedience to something larger than His own human needs, fears, and idiosyncrasies. Jesus had been told, just as the rest of us are, to be a good little boy, to sit up straight, to be nice, to study, to make His parents proud, to be successful. Like anyone else, Jesus had been told not to be bad, not to pull His sister's hair, not to play when He should be working, not to fail. He'd been told what to be and what not to be. Like anyone else, some of what He had accumulated over thirty years of living would help Him—and some of it wouldn't. So, before Jesus could truly carry out the work of someone who will heal the world, Jesus had to face this human struggle. He had to determine who he would be. Just as we do.

The Enemy comes to Jesus when Jesus is vulnerable—hungry, thirsty, alone—and makes Jesus look deep at His own Shadow, and offers Him ways to live that seem like good ideas at first. This is a test. A big one.

First, the Enemy asks Jesus to break His fast and turn stones to bread. It's a good suggestion. You're hungry. There's nothing wrong with eating. God never told us not to eat. Who's it gonna hurt? But Jesus recognizes this struggle as being about what you live on, what gets you through. If your primary objective is to keep yourself full—through consuming or stuffing yourself to make sure your empty places can't talk to you—you're going to avoid the spiritual path. Jesus had to stay on the spiritual path, even though, as is true for any other human being, that took a lot of effort.

The Russian novelist Dostoevsky suggests, too, that the temptation experience is all about the nature of power and Jesus' struggle with how to handle power. In the case of this first test, you're about to start a move-ment that you think will reach a lot of people. You want them to listen to what you have to say. A great way to reach them is through meeting their physical needs. Feed them. Promise them better roads, lower taxes. They'll love it. But Jesus decides that that's not what He wants His campaign to be about. Later, whenever large crowds of people want to make Him a political and religious guru, He sneaks away from them—literally. He doesn't want to be king; He wants to be a teacher. So, to stay centered in His response to the first test, Jesus quotes the Old Testament scripture that says that people don't live off of food alone, but are sustained by knowing God.

End of lesson one. Jesus has just figured something out about who He is and what He is struggling with. And He's determined one part of what He is and is not going to be. There is a part of any human being that would like for people to like us, to make us king or queen or ruler of the universe. Jesus struggles with this, too. But, unlike the rest of us, Jesus gets it right. That doesn't mean He won't ever feed people; He does. A few times He feeds thousands and thousands of people in one afternoon. But He decides here that if He's going to accomplish His mission, His ministry overall can't be about feeding people miraculously; it has to be about knowing God. And that's not something that you can do if you keep expecting a Big Mac to appear at your feet.

So the Enemy tries something else. The second temptation. "Why don't you throw yourself off the top of the highest tower in town? The angels will catch you, since you're the one God has sent to save the whole world, or whoever it is you think you are." [The point of testing in the desert is to ask Jesus that question: Who do you think you are? It's the biggest question for us as well. Jesus has to decide His own answer to that question.] This second test refers to the struggle about whether to get God to do miracles for you. You're in the desert. It sucks. You're tired and broken and lost. It would be really great if God would pull something majestic and get you out of this.

A parking place when you're at the back of the mall is nice; I know people who pray for parking places to open up closer to the store so they won't have to walk so far. Or maybe you want God to fix it for you when you're about to take a geometry exam that you're not really confident about. *Come on, God, help me take this test.* I taught in a maximum-security prison for three years, and one night an inmate who was really into the ministry at the unit said to me as I was passing out test papers, "I'm ready to take this test, teacher. Didn't study! Don't need to! The Holy Spirit has all knowledge and I know He'll see me through!" Later when I was grading the tests, I had to suppress the urge to write on his mangled, incoherent paper, *Tell the Holy Spirit to work on His grammar next time.*

Someone gets sick in the hospital, and you want God to perform a miracle for him or her. You get into deep trouble, and you need the universe to bail you out. You hit the wall and say, "God, how could you let this happen to me? You did this to me. Now fix it." This is another moment in which Jesus has to decide what His work is going to be about. The Grand Inquisitor in Dostoevsky's *The Brothers Karamazov* says that this test reflects human beings' wish to be admired and loved. Do great miracles. Do something amazing. Blow people away. Then everyone will want to follow you around. Of course this sounds like a good idea. You want to follow the miraculous. A sports hero who can fly through the air. A movie star whose big handsome head floats above us on the screen, kissing his beautiful co-star.

Jesus decides not to be a movie star. He also decides not to use God's power for silly or unimportant tasks. That doesn't mean that Jesus doesn't use God's power; He uses it frequently to heal, walk on water, even bring people who are dead back to life. But, like the miracles Jesus uses to feed people, the healings and supernatural acts that Jesus performs are never about show—they're always about healing or reassuring. They're intended to mend what is broken, not build Jesus' resume. Most of the time He does something amazing, He either disappears afterward or instructs those who've seen it not to tell anyone.

Jesus reminds the Enemy that the scriptures say we're not to test God in frivolous ways; God is Mystery, not a miracle vending machine. Is it wrong to ask God to give you a good parking place? Well, it's tricky. The Scriptures say that we are to ask God for whatever we need, but also that God doesn't usually give us what we want. God doesn't really bargain.

The soul doesn't bargain either. The soul is not reasonable. It doesn't care about your agenda. Working so hard to build your empire—which could be anything—that you develop migraines or hemorrhoids or eating disorders or rage or depression? Your soul is talking to you: "Rest, or your body will demonstrate how sick you're becoming." But we say, *Oh, I don't have to play by any rules. I'm Superman, Wonder Woman. I can do amazing feats of strength. I can keep going forever. I can throw myself off the highest tower, and my own achievements/excellence/prestige/status will catch me.* If you're a slacker rather than an achiever, it's actually the same thing: *I don't have to get a good job—or any job—or take responsibility for myself. I don't feel like finishing school or getting myself together. I like playing video games and chatting on IM. I like hanging out. I like being one of the guys in* Swingers. *I'll worry later. Insurance? Who needs it. I'll live forever.* It's the same thing. Dare the universe to make you human.

And it will. Everyone gets sick someday. It'll be you or someone you love. Reality will either fall down all around you like a big bad wolf blowing down your house of straw, or it will gently ease up closer and closer to you like a demon lover, till she's got you by the aorta, and then it'll be too late, and you'll just be a limited, foolish human being like the rest of us. If you've been relying on some miracle to save you, it will really suck when you hear yourself hit the pavement.

Jesus decides not to make His work about His fame as a miracle-worker. End of lesson two. Jesus has just figured out another thing about who He is and what He's decided to be.

I don't know if there were literally three questions the Enemy asked Jesus over a forty-day period, if he only asked each one once, if they were rolling around in Jesus' head for years, or what. But the books of Matthew and Luke say that the three tests are these three questions that represent the things Jesus was tempted to, and maybe in some way, like the rest of us, wanted to, be. His Enemy knows that. In the third test, Jesus' Enemy shows Jesus all the kingdoms of the world. He says, "I'll give you all this if you'll simply bow down and worship me."

It seems like a no-brainer; of course the answer is, *No, of course I would never bow to you. I choose to serve God.* But think about your own life. How many things do you serve? Let's go to the desert and be honest. The desert isn't about guilt. It's about honesty. There's no need to beat yourself up for your sins or to lift yourself up because of all your good deeds. In the desert, there's nobody to see you either way. So just tell the truth and examine it objectively. There's nobody else here. I know that's hard. You're conditioned to do exactly the opposite your whole life. But to be a healthy person and to be able to touch people and care for them, you've got to know who you really are, without guilt or self-importance.

Think about what you give yourself to; that's what you serve. Nearly everyone in our culture is dedicated to a God Jesus refers to as Mammon, a near-Eastern mythological term for greed. The pursuit of things and riches. Jesus said, "Spiritually and physically, it's impossible to be a slave owned by two masters at the same time. You can't serve both of them. In the end, it's one or the other." In order to be on a truly spiritual path, you have to know what your ultimate motive is. In this part of His temptation, the story says that Jesus is digging down into knowing what His own ultimate motive is.

But what's wrong with being politically shrewd? What's wrong with making a lot of money, if I do good things with it and keep a healthy perspective? Shouldn't I try to gain influence so that we can make a difference? That's a really sneaky thing about the way the Enemy confronts Jesus. Your own Shadow does this to you. Jesus was supposed to get people to follow Him, right? So what would have been so horrible about impressing them with meeting their needs or doing miracles for them? Wouldn't it have been great if Jesus had been able to amass political power and used governments and social systems as a way to help people be members of the Church?

The things that the Enemy offers to Jesus don't seem necessarily evil. They can honestly be seen as good things. That's perhaps some of why the tradition says that the Devil can take on a pleasing form. Knowing the difference between what's really best and what just feels best is tricky. It's especially tricky for the postmodern world, because the last few generations were all about getting what felt best.

But Jesus carries God's presence within Him. Jesus knows the difference. He concludes this last test by saying, "The Scriptures say, we are to love God and nothing else. Get away from me, Satan!" And He's passed this test as well. This was the final test, at least for now—the story says, "And so the Devil left him until a more opportune time." [The next times the Devil will attack, it'll be through Jesus' best friends, Simon Peter and Judas.]

Look at how each character in every story handles power. In *The Lord of the Rings,* the ring of power has a different effect on each person who interacts with it, depending on what's inside them. The Elf Queen Galadriel is offered the ring and resists the temptation—rather than becoming what she calls "a Queen, dark and terrible like the sea," she refuses to accept the ring and says, "I passed the test." The wizard Gandalf refuses even to touch the ring. Jesus does, too.

So why doesn't Jesus use the tools He's offered as a way to get through to people and build a worldwide church? Because He's not interested in creating what we think of as success. Jesus had a group of three close friends, nine other students, and a few hundred followers. That's whom He chose to instruct. He avoided crowds. He discouraged people from trying to follow Him. He refused to become the king of Israel. Yet that's what Christians are always trying to do: Make Jesus king of the world and tell everyone who doesn't belong to their kingdom that they have to die.

It's human nature to want to build a big, impressive movement, construct cathedrals and church buildings—or office buildings, castles, armies, huge governments, and gigantic church structures. We can't help it. We're like little boys building towers. The postmoderns are supposed to be disinterested in that because we've seen that human institutions are ultimately flawed and unreliable. But even so, we're impressed with miracle and power. At non-traditional, postmodern church conferences, nearly everyone's talking about strategies for building great things for God in the twenty-first century. It's just deep in the genes.

Jesus keeps warning against the deep desire within all of us to build something great. Yes, He is reported at the end of one of the versions of His ministry as telling His followers to go out and make disciples of all nations. But to be a disciple of someone who consistently refused to use power or influence doesn't mean to go out and tell people that they have to join the big successful institution—or else be punished for not obeying. A church marquee reading, "JESUS IS LORD: BOW OR BURN," some-how doesn't convey the love and self-sacrifice of Christ. Making disciples, if you follow Jesus' model, doesn't mean building a church; it means serving the poor and forgiving the broken. It means going into the desert and then coming back out and giving people some good news. It means that you're on a path centered on the spirit, and not the limited human agenda.

Saying, *I'm right, everybody else is going to hell, so memorize my answer and you'll avoid being kicked out,* is a nice, comforting formula which precludes the need for anyone to go into any desert. *The desert is where the Devil lives; don't go out there. Stay here in the fortress. Stay here with us. We've got God in here, too. We're obviously right.* Being part of a gigantic fortress—whether it's a corporation or church or government or economic empire—doesn't have anything to do with going to the desert. It's an antidote to going to the desert. It's the way out of the desert before you've gone through the desert. If you're rich and powerful and right, you don't ever have to actually feel anything. That's what Jesus refuses to do in His desert experience. But we're too human; we lack Jesus' larger perspective. We do it anyway.

Jesus' prayer that He taught the men and women in His school later included the phrase, "Lead us not into temptation—but deliver us from evil." It's as if He's saying, *God, we don't want to be tested. There's a part of us that wants to stay away from it. And putting You—or ourselves—to arbitrary tests is foolish. The spiritual life is not about us proving how tough we are. But when it is necessary that your Spirit send us into our own testing experiences, then help us, keep us from complete destruction.* He knows what it's like. The thing that helped Him grow is His own temptation experience. It could have destroyed Him, but it didn't. Jesus faced what He himself, like any other human being, longed for deep within—to be adored, followed, worshiped—by also facing the other side of what He longed for, which was to follow God and build something that would give His followers a truly transforming, saving path to follow.

Mark's Gospel says that at the end of the forty days in the wilderness with the wild beasts and the Enemy, the angels came to Jesus and served Him. That means that He won. The cosmic struggle He was part of turned out okay. He made it. Just making it through the desert is a victory. And, yes, there would be more temptations for Jesus, just as there are for us. But His desert experience made Him stronger, made Him discover who He was and what He had to reject in His own humanness and in the human agendas and fears of those around Him. We have to do that same thing. That's what Jesus calls His followers to do. Suffer. Struggle. Walk a difficult road. Wrestle. And out of that struggle with our own Enemy, we decide—maybe it has to be over and over—what we want to carry with us out of the desert and who we want to be. It's not about being "good." It's about being real. Jesus was offered good things—power, influence, success. He was reminded that He was beloved of God. These are all good things. But Jesus decided not to carry those things with Him out of the desert. He decided to let them go, and to walk on, to be clear in His purpose, not to need those things. And He travels on.

You are finally honest in the desert. You see your own fears, joys, pleasures, and tendencies. It is just who you are. As long as you beat yourself up for being human or deny that you are broken and limited, you remain stuck. But the healing path is about telling the truth, about continuing to travel. What do you want to continue to carry? What do you want to leave here? You discover who you are—and your course grows clearer and more purposeful. Not knowing who you are and not knowing what to keep or reject is part of what your Enemy wants. But you are on your path. You learn. You keep walking.

Here's one more desert story; it's like Jesus', and mine, and many other people's. Maybe it's like yours too.

Luke Skywalker, a sweet little orphan growing up out on the moisture farm on a desert planet [think about it—that's got to be one of the most impossible jobs in the galaxy] is a lot like Dorothy in *The Wizard of*

WELCOME TO THE DESERT

Oz. Luke longs to go over the rainbow and see something besides sand and sky. He wants to be a pilot and fly—like the bluebirds that fly in Dorothy's song. Something in him wants to know who he really can be. And he knows it isn't to be found around here.

So fate, the gods, whatever—in George Lucas' universe, it's the Force—sends him messengers from the sky to invade his safe little world and tell him who he is. A wise teacher, old Ben Kenobi, comes and guides him to the larger world. *You aren't just a kid from nowhere. You are the son of the greatest Jedi Knight of all. You have a destiny. The Force needs you.*

Well, so far, it sounds great. I'm getting off of this dust ball and I'm going on a great adventure. And the original *Star Wars* in 1977 is that kind of adventure. Sweet, exciting, and mythic, it's all about youth, hope, and literally and spiritually flying. When the movies were later re-numbered, Lucas titled it *Star Wars Episode IV: A New Hope*. It's all about hope. Luke meets adversity and gets to blow up the Death Star and defeat the evil Empire. So who wouldn't want to be part of that? There's no broken-ness required for that kind of path. You get to stay young.

Lucas understands the deepest myths, the deepest part of what Americans—and everyone else—struggle with: ego. We're certainly not the first group of human beings to deal with this issue; this is old stuff. These stories have been told a million times in every culture. But for us postmoderns, the issue is even more critical, because we're not hopeful. We were becoming a very jaded culture in the mid-seventies. So first, to get people to buy his story, Lucas had to enchant us. Our culture is so frag-mented and shallow that we have very little hope in anything. So Lucas wooed us with this wonderful fairy tale all about the happy story of the young warrior hero who goes on this adventure with his merry band, saves the universe, and tosses the villain out into the darkness.

Luke's adventure continues in *The Empire Strikes Back,* only now things get darker. The title tells you that up front. Now Luke and his friends aren't part of a quickie adventure; they're officers in a war. It goes on for years. Put yourself in Luke's position. It's hard work; you go from one desert to another—sand, snow, clouds. And then it gets worse. You are separated from your friends, and so you go to meet another wise teacher and get some guidance.

This teacher doesn't look like anything you expected. He's a little, grumpy green thing. Not thrilling or sexy at all. And while you're ready to race off into the sky to rescue everyone, what does he try to teach you? Patience. Peacefulness. Control. Focus. Prayer.

You don't have any of that. You hate it. It's boring. You want to go be the hero again, go find your friends, go defeat the bad guy who killed your famous, wonderful, royal father, and get the princess. The little teacher warns you that your father was just the same, and he ended up destroyed because of it. But you don't care. You are an adolescent. You are post-1960 sitcom America. You are the teenager with a huge dose of the Force at your disposal. Why would you want discipline? You want to be tested, so we can all see how powerful you are. You want to go grab all the gusto, be all you can be, go for it, just do it—fill in the advertising slogan you prefer. Ride 'em cowboy.

Yoda tries to get through to you by sending you on a vision quest. You go deep into the swamp, another kind of desert wilderness. There's a lesson there for you. The desert is where you learn and suffer. [The beautiful, sophisticated, serene cities or planets, like the cloud city Bespin in *Empire* or the capital city-planet Coruscant in *The Phantom Menace* and *Attack of the Clones* are actually where the greatest corruption and blindness are.]

Yoda tells you that you won't need your weapons, but you can't help it. You take your lightsaber anyway. You want your phallic symbol, your gun, your glass of wine, your bazooka, your S.U.V., your money, your new toy, your well-supported doctrine or philosophy—whatever you think makes you invincible.

You go out, away from camp. You are among the wild beasts, the snakes and the hidden things, just like Jesus and John the Baptist. You go alone. And what you find when you go into the deep dark place—in this story, it's a cave—is a giant monster, dressed in black, all machine and menace and coldness. This is terrifying. This is a power and mystery you can't control or get a handle on. This is the dragon, Grendel, savages, Indians, the Communists, the Taliban.

You draw your weapon and strike—and what you see in the fallen helmet is your own face. Your own limitations. Your own sickness. Your own addictions. Your own lies. Your own humanity. Every great enemy shows us the dark side of who we are. The real question is whether we'll learn anything.

This experience in the cave *nearly* gets your attention. But you say to Yoda, "I'm gone. I'm out of here. I've faced my fears and I'm off to save the day." Yoda tries to talk you out of it, but you're not having any. You're not broken enough yet.

At the end of the movie, you and Darth Vader are face-to-face, man to monster. You think you can beat him. You attack. You've gotten stronger and tougher, and you fight hard. He tells you to channel all that hatred at him. After all, you're the holy knight on the quest to kill the dragon that killed your king. You are righteous. You are Beowulf, Aragorn, Batman, Mel Gibson, Samuel L. Jackson, Charlie's Angels, John Wayne. Kick his butt. Show him who's boss.

But unlike comic book heroes, you can't win. The harder you fight, the more desperate you become. And so, since you can't control your fears yet—you haven't spent enough time in the desert—the monster beats you, and to make sure you understand that this is real, Lucas has Vader cut your right hand off.

As I mentioned before, I bet you know people who have ascended too fast and who have hit the wall. They weren't ready yet. Maybe you've done the same thing. I was in such a hurry to grow up and build my career that when I got married and started out, not making very much money and then having a baby soon after that, and having to teach more evening classes to make more money so we could build a house to put our little family in, I got burned out. I hadn't learned enough yet. I wanted it all. But I learned that I wasn't ready for it all. I have a good friend who did the opposite. He went right out of law school, got a job with a well-established firm, never lost a case, became the golden boy. Made loads of money. Belonged to the old money country club in town. Played golf three or four times a week, drove a new extended cab pickup truck, bought a beautiful house. I was so jealous. This guy had it all. I went to see him a few years into his practice and asked him how it was going and tears came to his eyes. "I don't know how I'm going to make it," he said. [And I saw my own Shadow—my own jealousy and ambition—rise up in front of me.] I asked him what was wrong and he said, "The pressure to perform is so huge that everybody here drinks all the time. We work ridiculous hours. We have no life. I've had a lot of women, but I'm never going to find anybody to settle down with because I can't invest in anybody long enough to build anything that will last. I thought this was what I wanted." Isn't it? I thought to myself—not about my friend, but about me.

When you fly out so fast without having learned anything, the monster waiting for you shows you that you're not so wonderful after all. You can be beaten. And you know what else? That thing that you thought was the enemy? It's you.

"Luke," he says, "I am your father." *I am your destiny. I'm what you're made of. You're sick, too, just like me. You're full of hate, too, just like me. You're corrupt, too, just like me. Welcome to the club.*

Now it's hitting you. The brokenness. Now you're there. There's nowhere to go from here. This is a tornado lifting the entire galaxy off the ground and dumping it somewhere over the rainbow. This is the desert. If this doesn't get your attention, probably nothing else will. You'll die old and unenlightened, retired in the suburbs, complaining about how things didn't go your way and how the paper doesn't get thrown where you think it should on the driveway.

"Why didn't you tell me?" You say accusingly to your wise teachers, trying to blame this crisis on them. Their answer? "We did try to tell you, you headstrong jerk, but you wouldn't listen!" You are like every other foolish young man or woman, focused only on achieving and running away from themselves.

You run from Vader, and you're rescued by the girl you love, so it's okay for the moment. But you lie there, beaten, with no right hand, knowing something will never be the same. Part of you is dead. This was definitely a kind of baptism. Welcome to the desert.

Something happens between the second movie and its sequel, the final one in the series, *Return of the Jedi*. You have settled down and begun some real soul-searching. Now you've given up your ambition. You've learned to be still. This will lead you to your real power. And it's not physical power, it's not being the prettiest or the fastest or the richest. Those things are all about the Empire. Instead, you go the way of spiritual journey and discipline. And you go deeper and deeper.

Meanwhile, it's 1983 and audiences around the world anxiously await the movie's release. The name of the movie, *Return of the Jedi*, makes them think, *Hey, excellent—a Jedi army! Yeah! Finally! The Empire is going to get it now, boy!* But Lucas is way ahead. They're still in an adolescent mind; Luke is in Jedi mind, spirit-mind, I've-been-to-the-desert mind. In *Return of the Jedi*, there's only one Jedi. Only one. Yoda dies. Obi-Wan Kenobi is already dead. The only one who remains is Luke. That's who returns. But this entire series of movies is his story, so that's all that matters.

The price you've had to pay is enormous, Luke, but there is victory at the end of this part of the story. You had to travel a long way. You studied. You prayed. You trained. You went back to Yoda and started over and over. When Yoda was satisfied that you were ready, he passed on the legacy to you. You learned discipline and focus. You became the most powerful warrior of all. Lucas is teaching: You give it all up. You surrender, without giving in or compromising who you are. That's real power. That's the cross. That's the path that leads to enlightenment, salvation, healing.

When Luke finally confronts Darth Vader in the end of the saga,

Episode VI, he returns not as an avenging army, but as a son who has come to surrender to the monster in the hope of helping the monster become whole. In the supreme act of strength, Luke gives up. He relinquishes his power rather than kill his father, the monster he's been fighting all this time.

Shouldn't you destroy him? When he first sees you again, he tries to draw you out, to make you fight—-and you start to. You want to. You cut his hand off just like he cut off yours. Serves him right. But then you realize that he, too, is broken. He missed it. He had hope and power and goodness within [We find out in *Episode I* that he was the greatest channel of The Force, the greatest spirit-warrior anyone had ever seen], but he blew it. And not because he was the dragon, not because he was evil, but simply because he was human. Just an imperfect person like anybody else, who had great dreams and, instead of learning how to tame his ambition, fulfilled his dreams, and so thereby caused his own doom.

George Lucas has said in a number of interviews that the problem with Anakin, Luke's father who becomes Darth Vader, is attachment. "He turns into Darth Vader because he gets attached to things. He can't let go of his mother; he can't let go of his girlfriend. He can't let go of things. It makes you greedy. And when you're greedy, you are on the path to the dark side, because you fear you're going to lose things, that you're not going to have the power you need."⁵ This idea—found in all great religious traditions, including Christianity, is that whatever you're attached to needs to go. The more you demand that you hold something tight, that it belongs to you, the more you become enslaved by it. It doesn't matter what the thing is—it can be anything. It doesn't have to be a *thing* at all. It can be jealousy, a grudge, territory, ambition, possessions, appetite: all the things that you can't carry with you into the desert.

5 Richard Corliss and Jess Cagle, "Dark Victory: An Inside Look at the New 'Star Wars' Episode: How the Young Darth Vader Fell In Love and George Lucas Rediscovered the Heart and Soul of His Epic Series," *Time*, April 19, 2002: 64.

Jesus, too, talks about this problem, in the image of the rich man and the eye of a needle, and also in a striking metaphor that, probably not coincidentally, is reminiscent of the hand-cutting-off motif in the men of *Star Wars*: Jesus tells His students, "If your right hand makes you sin, cut it off. If your right eye makes you sin, pull it out. If your right foot causes you to sin, cut it off." And I bet the disciples are thinking, *What has happened to Him? He was already so hard to understand— and now this? Is He serious?*

Jesus isn't literally advocating physical self-mutilation; He's using symbolic, shocking language, as He does often, to get His point across. He adds: "It's better to enter the Kingdom missing a body part than to be in what looks like great shape and end up with your soul destroyed." What leads to sin? Anything we refuse to let go of. The desert is the place for stripping small things away in order to find the bigger things, the real things.

It's Anakin's refusal to let go that's the problem. It convinces him to insist on being the leader of the army that becomes the weapon of the Empire. And it will lead him to his own physical and emotional crippling. That's why he has to wear the black suit and the breathing mask. When Luke confronts his father in the final movie, he begins to realize this about Darth Vader, *This is what turned my father the Jedi into Darth Vader: he couldn't let go. He became enslaved.* You can't defeat that enslavement with more power, more enslavement. Instead of "giving in to hate" as the stories say many times, Luke chooses ... surrender and brokenness.

It's a lesson his father finally grasps as well. Anakin dies, but not before he is healed. He releases his power, refuses to kill his son, kills his master, the Emperor, instead, and dies. And so he's okay. Goodness and peace can return to the galaxy, not because of victory, ascending, power, achievement—but because of true love and surrender. Luke is willing to sacrifice himself out of love for his father and for his friends. And Darth Vader dies, but the now-redeemed spirit of Anakin, the great knight within the monster, lives on.

Luke doesn't even get the girl. His rowdy best friend does. The girl happens to be his sister, so even though teenagers seeing the movie were horrified that he'd ever had a crush on her, it makes sense. The adolescent view of everything—including sexual conquest and "falling in love" isn't the point; that would be a distraction. It's something you grow out of. Luke has a different job to do. He loves the princess and defends her not out of lust but out of his soul. They are siblings, twin royal children, who restore their kingdom through love and bravery.

The adolescent wants to be a king. But he cannot ascend until he has gone on his journey downward, into the desert.

We want to be happy and successful. But we will not have joy until we relinquish control and learn the power of brokenness and surrender. That is what Jesus experiences in His temptation. That is what it means to wander out in the wilderness.

I think that to a certain extent our entire culture is in a time when it's possible that we could begin a meaningful journey into the desert. We're already on the brink. So much of the stuff that characterized our childhood as a culture has been stripped away. The tornado has come and picked up our house and thrown it around—that was going on the entire last century. There have been a series of awakenings and things dying. There's some potential there for a desert walk.

But we resist. We're like a child, like the young Luke. There is a part of us that wants to leave the crumbling fortress and ride out onto the prairie. But there is also that civilized part of us that sees security in knowing the answers and following the rules. *If the building crumbles, where are the answers now? Who am I? How did I get here? Where do I go from here?* Our culture is in that moment. I think it has been for fifty years, which isn't a long time as far as the development of an empire is concerned. I think we are in a particular place in that journey. We're in the midst of that series of critical moments in which we're shown that we're not perfect, that we don't know all the answers, that we don't have it all together. That part of the truth about us is that we're liars, just like everybody else. We're cheats. We're full of rage. We don't want anyone else to be happy.

But it's also true that we are full of worth. We are beloved of God—just like everybody else. What will we do with this awareness? To answer that question is the universal desert experience. And what happens is that we either accept that we're not perfect and strip all the artifice and pretense away, go naked, be open, or we rebuild the walls. We say, "No, I have to be the hero. Thanks, Yoda, but I've got to fly away and save my friends and destroy evil. There's nothing wrong with me." *I am America, or Russia, or England, or the Roman Empire, or Christianity, or whatever other empire you belong to. Everything is beautiful, especially me.*

No. The way Jesus defeats his Enemy is to trust that He isn't alone. God, it turns out, came with Him. He is still a son of God, even out in the desert. That didn't change. He trusts something. And He therefore continues His journey, and leaves the desert, according to the story, "full of the Spirit of God."

America doesn't trust anything. We're hanging in there, and that's good. We believe in some basic things that we were told all along, and, like the basic lessons that a child is taught, those things are good to know and remember. But adulthood is also about facing what isn't right, what the theories don't teach about. It's not about trust; it's about control. We're still controlling every freaking thing. We're too afraid to let go. So we keep building little and big walls. My race is better. My religion is better. My money is better. My body is better. My sexuality is better. My denomination is better. My yard is better. My city is better. My football team is better. My way of seeing things is better. But, in a win-lose situation within a family, everybody loses. We haven't figured that out yet. We still want to be the big winner. We still want to defeat everyone else. But everyone is our family.

The attacks of September 11, 2001 should make us realize that we're not Superman. Not only are we not perfectly safe, we're not perfect. If someone hates us this much, is it possible that something isn't right overall? Is it possible that we have contributed to the world as being an unhealthy place? We didn't deserve to be attacked. But we're not blameless either. What the September 11 experience has made so many people feel is that we're much more right and righteous than everyone else in the world, and that everybody else, especially the people who've made us mad, are all evil, the Devil, whatever. That's not the Spirit that drove us to the desert talking; that's the Empire talking.

We're on the edge of the desert in our culture. We have the opportunity to head in, strip naked, find out the truth, and trust something. But we're afraid. And a part of us wants to turn back. We're afraid that if we head out into the truth, there won't be anything there, and the whole risk will have been a waste. So we waver. And wait. And avoid the real journey.

But what if, in our desert experiences, we find a way not to run, not to avoid the truth, and not to fool or distract ourselves? What if, at the end of our marriages, for example, we decide to do real soul-searching as a way to figure out who we are and what happened? What if we don't run from our own Shadows, but decide to wrestle with them and see what it is we're so afraid of? What if we stop, just before taking the big promotion, and really pray and listen to our souls to see if that's what they really want and long for?

The trouble is that it's terrifying to face what's inside you. Demons are in there. Hidden things. Voices that keep echoing off the walls, old tapes that you can hear playing and rewinding over and over somewhere back in the darkness. Your Enemy waits to confront you about your own appetites and desires for power or control. A monster is hiding under the bed, or in a cave, or behind you. A dragon rustles out in the forest, just beyond the clearing.

Any system or formula for avoiding really facing this dark thing is ultimately not going to work. At some point, we just have to acknowledge that there is what Hamlet calls, "the undiscovered country" that everybody is afraid of. In his case, he thinks his enemy is death, but it's really his own fear. I think maybe that's everybody's.

According to one of the Christian scriptures, the thing that "casts out fear" is "perfect love." Love. Love is the thing that gives us courage. It makes us strong. It makes us able to reach beyond our own limited, fearful, "sinful" hearts. How do we love? By trusting something.

TRUST SOMETHING

CHAPTER_5

I Chose To Walk Out Here, But Now I'm Stuck

It's difficult, but you awaken. Maybe it takes a crisis or something like a tornado to get the process going. You start the journey, and before long, you're traveling into the desert to discover who you are and what matters. The big question now is: How am I going to survive this, and then what happens?

I think I can do this on my own. That's all I have anyway. My grandparents and their generation of bankers and community volunteers don't understand my disconnection from their culture. My parents unplugged from the world they grew up in, but they were busy chasing their own happiness and gathering stuff and status. They don't understand why I don't want what they have. And the culture they've helped create is a mess. This has left me wounded and cynical. I keep my dreams to myself and hang out with my friends. I'm still somehow hopeful, but I distrust a lot, so I take care of myself and watch out for stupid things.

But toughness isn't enough to make it through the desert. To survive this cleansing and focusing process, it really helps to trust somebody or something. But trusting is very hard to do. And that's not just something that's true of the twenty-first century; it's always been against people's nature to let go.

It's dangerous to love. It's dangerous to feel anything; it hurts too much. And it's dangerous to be vulnerable. For my grandparents, to be emotionally or spiritually vulnerable means you're wimpy. Men didn't cry. People didn't go around making a fuss about something just because they had this or that feeling. Suck it up. After all, the things you are trained to trust are the same institutions everyone trusts. For my parents, trusting something other than yourself wasn't the point. The point was achieving, finding your way, making your career. That took a lot of self-determination. In the sixties you had the revolutions to fight and win; in the seventies it was time to go on your emotional journey and get yourself together; in the eighties and nineties it was time to make some money and build your empire. None of that involved opening up to anything other than yourself.

There's a church in Portland, Oregon, called The Bridge. Its members and clergy have many piercings and tattoos. Some have shaved heads and others have dreadlocks. They wear lots of black and clothes from the Salvation Army thrift store. A few months ago, I was talking to two of the adults who are leaders of that church, and they talked about how the people who are part of that community—they don't call it a "church" necessarily—find it very hard to trust anybody, especially God. The main reason is because they've been screwed over by their families and their families' values. Their parents were emotionally unavailable one way or another—whether they were moneyed or poor, strict disciplinarians or totally absent. The leaders of The Bridge told me that Portland has the highest per capita percentage of homeless teenagers and young adults of any major city in America. And at least 60 percent of those kids were raised in Bible-believing, Christian homes. Something went wrong.

I think that these kids on the streets are, in some ways, the ones who are telling the truth for all the ones out there—millions of them, I think—who are also emotionally wounded and cut off, but who look more normal than the kids at The Bridge. They've found a way to fit in, even though in their hearts they may not at all. Many people under thirty-five are emotionally and spiritually closed down. They've found ways to drown out the pain. That's nothing new. A captain in the Army in 1924 didn't get to sit around and talk about his feelings; he just dealt with it. Women in the Depression didn't have the luxury of getting in touch with things; the poor ones just did their kids' and husbands' laundry, and the rich ones went to teas and were polite.

But there is something specifically urgent and painful about the mistrust and distance that hunker down in the hearts of postmoderns, and they carry the signs of it, whether internally or externally. I think it's that they just don't have anything else. My friend Bennett, who is in his seventies, grew up in a very emotionally distant home. Nobody said they loved you or that they were proud of you, but they'd let you know if you'd displeased or disappointed them. Bennett, who was the oldest son, fought with his cold, quiet father all the time, and then at seventeen, left home, enlisted in the Navy, and never moved back home. He lives in Austin now that he's retired, but that's still a long way from the little town in Texas that he came from. But, unlike a twenty-five year old today who also feels cut off from a solid foundation, Bennett had two things that kept him from thinking he was completely crazy and alone in the universe. He had the as-yet-still-trustworthy institutions of his culture. The Navy. The government—whether you believed in all it stood for or not, you knew it was there. The Church. The moral code of right and wrong. And beyond that, he also had no real expectation of emotional intimacy in the first place. I mean, of course he'd had hope in his heart when he was seven that his parents would love him and approve of him. Everybody's born wanting the blessing. But for someone born before 1940, you were just told to put up with it whether you got it or not. That's how it was. People over sixty-five have told me that in some ways, that made it easier. I find that very few people in that generation want to open up too far, at least unless they know you very deeply. [The women seem to open up more easily than the men do, but I think that that's how it is in every culture I know of in the Western world.]

I'm not suggesting that everyone born before 1970 had it easy and felt secure. That's simply not true. There have always been horrible amounts of racism, sexism, poverty, suffering, abuse. There still are, even in America, the richest country in the history of human civilization. I'm not suggesting that life before punk rock was tidy and happy. Rather, what I'm suggesting is that there is a particular burden that the present generation has inherited, a burden which the people for the last hundred years before us did not have to carry. Ours is a generation—not the first in history, certainly, and not unlike others, the children raised during wartime in any culture, being an example—who don't have any real basis of security or overall meaning provided by their culture.

However, we are also one of the few cultures in history to be free to choose everything we want to believe in or value. Completely free. Those in charge of answers and truth have conceded that there are many valid answers, and you can just pick the ones you like. There are no absolute rules, even though there are those we choose to retain from the many threads of previous cultural norms and traditions. Still, the point is, we are free to choose to retain them or go find our own.

This may not always feel like a gigantic blessing, but it can be. That kind of freedom can be like a free flight into the skies. Of course, it can also feel like a wild spiral across ground that's being rolled and pushed up and down by an earthquake.

The Boomers and post-Boomers—I'm going to generalize and say those born between 1940 and the late 1960s, in the midst of the old, modern world falling apart around their ears, found meaning in their quest to discover what was real within themselves. It's a generation in which the point of life was to find your own way through the maze of the world and get in touch with your feelings. The answer was a largely self-absorbed one. Their parents were often emotionally distant, too, but the Boomers found solace not in the institutions of their culture but in their own search for the Holy Grail of the Actualized Self. They don't trust much outside themselves; to depend on something larger would mean that it's not about me. Way too restricting.

Of course, that's not much of a superstructure underneath the building. Like children raised during a war, the children of the Boomers have trouble just relaxing and feeling safe—even the ones whose families were affection-ate and affirming. The security you've got is only as old as your parents. And that's not much to base an entire civilization on. But at least you were loved in the first place, so that's something.

However, if your parents were too into their own stuff—money, despair, toys, work, drugs, spirituality—to be there for you at all, you're out of luck. You're totally alone. Ultimately, you've got nothing. No government to trust. No church. No God. Any system or way of thinking is one that you didn't inherit, but have chosen on your own, because the foundation given to you wasn't trustworthy. That's a lot of responsibility to have to handle as a young person. It's a lot for *any* person. The weight of it makes some people sort of crazy. But if you were part of a system that said everything was good and that if you had questions or problems, you were crazy—then to get out of that system is sanity. And the openness that comes from freedom can make people determined to find something to believe in.

I talked to a twenty-year-old woman named Kelly, a very together person who came to The Bridge a year or so ago. She has a tongue stud, about six or seven earrings, and rings in her nose and in her eyebrow. A great tattoo of a dragon rises up out of the top of her torn T-shirt, slithering around her neck. She has stringy, uncombed black and orange hair. Her tennis shoes don't match. I think my great Uncle Weldon had the same kind of work pants she's wearing.

Kelly was born in a little town in Minnesota. Her father was an alcoholic. Her mother worked night shifts at the little diner in town. Her Grandma lived a mile or so away. Kelly went to school, like everybody else. They went to church sometimes. And stuff happened, some of it good and some of it not so good, just as it does to everybody else. She got into drugs. And other things. She didn't talk about all of it with me; I don't think she's told anyone all of it. When Kelly was sixteen, she left and hitch-hiked to Portland to live with her cousin. She got a job sacking groceries at a supermarket. She started using. She went to live with her dealer. After a few months he began beating her. So she left him too.

Kelly says that the reason she finds it hard to trust anything isn't because everyone is evil. "I know there are good people in the world," she says. "They just weren't in my family. So I got out. And ended up here." She's looking for a job. She laughs easily and has a shy smile. She's eighteen now. Her voice is husky, like Lauren Bacall's, made more so because she smokes constantly. She wears very black lipstick. And even though she tries not to show it, she has a baby face. Big eyes and eyelashes without wearing any mascara.

Of course she doesn't trust anybody. She tells me, blowing a long stream of smoke, "I hung out at the city shelter across that block over there for a while, but they sucked. Nobody that worked there gave a sh-t about any of us. They were just doing it for a paycheck." She shrugs.

"But, it was warm and it doesn't rain inside." She smiles, a kind gesture in the face of what she's already faced in her life. She smiles, and there is a kind of hopefulness in her eyes. She's strong. She keeps going even with what she's already had to face in her life.

I'm absolutely convinced that there are just as many people in the suburbs who are like Kelly as there are in the streets, but most of them look more or less normal. Everybody watches television. Everybody wishes they were thinner and more muscular. Everybody wonders what's going to happen next. Everybody's had a heart break. Everybody's afraid in some way or another. But the people in the suburbs and big city buildings have more resources—emotional, financial—to use in order to mask their emptiness or uncertainty. I've had so many people who look good open up to me to tell me how sad or angry they are. They're married or single, they have enough money or they don't, they fit in or they don't—it doesn't matter. Their kids are in soccer. They go to church, or belong to the PTA, or go on business trips. But they feel like Neo in *The Matrix*—there's something missing. Something wrong. They're wondering what there is to believe in, deep down. And it makes them feel sad or angry. A tornado will set it off and make them realize how little their house is. But it will also awaken something within them. The world starts to turn bright colors. And the Spirit drives them into the desert. But then what?

What do you say to Kelly? She's a tough woman. She's hung in there through a long road and lots of suffering. She's been to the desert—and bravely, rather than stay huddled in a valley somewhere, now she's going out even further, to find a new way to live. And she is in the process of coming out the other side, mostly because she's opened herself up enough to become part of the community at The Bridge. She's starting to seem okay. But when she smiles and lowers her eyes, she's telling me: I'm not okay yet. I'm scared. I've been in a lot of pain.

To trust would be weakness; her bones tell her that. Her bones also tell her that she would like to have something to trust. But it's risky. Too much has already let her down and hurt her. And yet something talks to her soul and says, *I am with you, even in this place, and I can be with you beyond this place.* And she, not unlike the rest of us, wants it to be true.

Nobody wants to trust, not naturally, not as soon as you're a six-month-old baby and you realize in the deepest part of your heart that your parents aren't going to be able to give to you unselfishly, or meet your needs with true love. It soaks in, that at some basic level you're on your own. So, for the rest of your life, you develop ways to cope and control your environment. You always feel broken and afraid in some way. I think that may be a large part of what the Bible calls "the sin of the world." It's not that you're evil because you do evil things; it's that you do broken things because you're broken and afraid.

You feel that if you do relax and trust someone, it may be okay. But you still keep your guard up, way down deep. Like Matt Damon's character in *Good Will Hunting*, you're afraid that if you open up and care about anything or love anything, you'll get burned again, just as you were when you were growing up and realized that your parents, teachers, pastors, or heroes, were all, at least in some ways, acting out of response to their own anger or weakness.

Wonderful people exist. Noble people. There are truly healthy human beings who've worked hard to make sense of their in-the-bones human fallibility, and find ways to be loving and giving anyway. But the older you get, the more you find that those healthy people are really rare. Over and over, you get burned and disappointed. So you become tough instead.

You're conditioned not to be vulnerable. It would mean giving up, passivity. Giving in. So instead, like Will Hunting, you hold everyone at a distance. Like Will, you long for connection and love but are afraid that only pain can follow being vulnerable. Instead of continuing your spiritual journey and learning to let go, you strap on your weapons and keep it together. And maybe you're really afraid of letting go of control so deeply that you never go to the desert in the first place. The desert means vulnerability. You're afraid that maybe you'll never get out of the desert at all. *If I can't take my weapons with me, I won't get to fight back.*

I personally have a lot of trouble trusting people, probably partly because I'm an optimist by nature. Growing up, I just trusted everybody and got burned by a few mean people. The girl I adored in high school dumped me. My best pal in junior high told me I had weird-shaped feet. The first boss I had out of college lied to me about my salary and benefits and then denied it. My parents divorced, and the floor always rolled a little after that. It's not a very impressive list, I know; you've probably got a better one. But it's just what people go through, especially the ones who are by nature hopeful, like I am.

So opening up is difficult, because I'm afraid I'll lose control, and I'll get hurt again. Trust feels passive. It feels like I'll be weak and I won't be "the man" anymore. This was a big problem for me in the first years of my marriage. I was defensive all the time. My poor wife would walk through the room while getting her bags packed, and ask if we had gas in the car before heading to her parents' for the weekend—and I'd blurt out something lovely like, "What makes you think I don't know how to fill the gas tank?" She'd walk off wondering what she'd done wrong. Maybe trust feels like weakness to men in general; we're so driven by ego and worry that we're not strong enough or smart enough. But it's hard, too, for me and for practically every other man I've ever talked to, to simply open up to a woman. I want to be in control. If I slow down at work or at home, I'll feel my own pain. I won't be strong. I might not know the answer. Actually, many women tell me they feel this way, too, so maybe it's not just a guy thing; maybe it's just a people thing.

The civilizations before us came up with lots of systems and tools with which to keep things under control. And it's tempting to go back to those when we feel insecure. Many people are still racists, sexists, control freaks, or money freaks. Many, many people in our culture can't let go. They keep grasping at whatever happens to be close by, so that they can be sure they don't have to open up. Feeling something real means that what happens to us or inside us might spin out of control and wreck what we've worked so hard to build, the seawall that holds back the tidal wave that surely waits out there, rumbling, scaring the crap out of us. As if we can hold back a tidal wave. But what if we surfed?

Surf The Desert

I went to high school in a city near the ocean, and when fall hurricane season came, all the surfers would wait every day for storms. The waves were pretty puny most of the time, so the surfers prayed for hurricanes. When a big storm came, the police would evacuate Padre Island as much as possible, and then close off the roads that led out to the beaches to keep the curious or foolish people from driving out to look at the storm. My buds would park out in the middle of nowhere and sneak over sand dunes with their boards under their arms to get out into the surf.

Some people have, somehow, figured out that to surrender is not, in fact, passive at all. To let go doesn't mean defeat; it can mean that we recognize that there are powerful spiritual and emotional tides that are all around us and within us, and decide to release and ride along. Life has gigantic swells and currents, so we try to build seawalls and barricades. Our emotional houses get bigger and stronger. Maybe we can survive for ten years, or fifty, or a hundred. Then, eventually, there will be a big enough storm to knock a few holes in the house—or just knock it over completely.

But Jesus talks about giving up the huge structure with lots of storage space and plenty of electronic toys in order to ride easy and be ready to move when the waves change. Surfing the waves seems more dangerous than staying safe and warm in the big house. But Jesus' point over and over is: We're not safe in our big houses anyway. That sense of stability and security is an illusion. So where is security? Strangely, it's on the waves.

A number of times in the Gospel stories, when Jesus encountered someone who was sick and wanted to be healed, Jesus asked them something like, "Do you really want to be healed?" or, "Do you believe that I can heal you?" When the person answered yes, Jesus then said, "Alright. Get up. Go on about your business." They were healed instantly. Everything was different. And then they'd look over at Jesus—everyone in the room—and He'd explain, "What made you whole—healed—was your own faith."

The usual interpretation of the phrase, "your faith has made you well," is that it refers to healing that comes from trust in the proposition that Christ is Lord and Savior. But I'm starting to think that Jesus may be saying that it's not magical, miraculous powers that can heal us, and it's not some mysterious knowledge we have, and it's not religion. What Jesus keeps saying is, "What made you well was the fact that you were willing to trust God. That's it. That's what made you well," He tells them. "All I did was open the window and let a little fresh air in, stand over here and get you to realize the door was unlocked all along. The Kingdom of God is already within you." Maybe the biggest spiritual issue is whether we'll let go of our own control of everything, and just trust that our fears and insecurities are not the center of the universe. God is bigger than we are. Everything's bigger than we are. We'd better trust something. Otherwise it's a large and lonely universe. Which, of course, for a twenty-first century person, it can be. If the modern way of knowing is based on knowing what is true because it's provable, then what about things that can't be proven? What if the mystery of our experience can't be explained? The control we thought we had becomes unraveled. We respond in fear.

That's nothing new; fairy tales a thousand years old are about the warrior who defends the village or castle from the ogre or dragon out in the darkness that carries away our sheep. So here we are in the midst of postmodern culture, with ogres right and left, outside and inside. We want to get big weapons and defend ourselves. Very modern. Very us versus them. Very "there must be a winner and a loser." But what if real strength is in saying, "I'm going to walk into the forest and see what happens. Yes, there are dangerous things there. But that's also where the treasure is. God is out there where I can't control what happens. I can't explain how Jesus will heal me. It terrifies me. But I believe it, in a deep, non-rational way. And then I become a new person—not all at once, but cell by cell, a half hour at a time."

Spiritual baptism isn't something we do; it's something God does. Yet we do something, too: We trust that we'll survive. My son is a swimmer. I've noticed that all he has to do is to lie flat, and he floats across the water, half in and half out. The best swimmers are the ones who make almost no splashes or waves; they're using the water, rather than fighting it. I picture Jesus walking on water as being like that: it's not like the smooth surface of glass; it's like something He rests on and in, like faith. It moves, and He moves with it. And then He goes faster.

We want an answer, but I'm not sure God is particularly interested in giving one—at least, not one that we can list, outline, and define. The story of Moses says that one day he is out tending to his sheep when he sees a shrub, the kind that stands around in the desert next to rocks or cracks in the dirt. The shrub is on fire. This isn't an uncommon occurrence, since the hot Middle Eastern sun sparked small, dry branches, and little bushes crackled and went up in small, unimportant flames between the boulders in the desert. But this shrub doesn't disappear in the few minutes it usually took for a little bush to give itself up to smoke and cinders; this one just keeps burning. And Moses notices.

As I suggested earlier in this book, at this moment, Moses is now awake. But it is not just that he is paying attention. Once you look around and see a larger world than you thought existed, there's even more. In this case, the shrub talks.

Obviously, it isn't the shrub talking. The burning-but-not-burning bush is a device God and Moses use together to have this meeting in which Moses has an experience of God's presence. The shrub talks, and Moses listens. He and what he understands as the God of his ancestors, the children of Israel, have a conversation. God gives Moses a job to do: Go and petition the king of Egypt to let the Israelites leave and go back to the land their ancestors left four hundred years ago.

It's a transforming moment. Moses will never be the same person. He has heard the voice of God, experienced the ultimate mystery.

What does he do? Moses is no oil painting icon, no Hollywood Charlton Heston. He is a complex, tainted, yet courageous human being, like almost everyone in the Bible, even though we've turned them into abstract saints and religious legends. What does Moses do in response to encountering the voice of God? He *argues* with God. So, if you've been resisting whatever it is that you feel God is doing in you, you're in good company.

This is Moses' wrestling in the desert, his test—one of them, anyway; there would be many more. [That's important to know, too: You don't necessarily travel into the desert once; you go over and over—another reason to learn to trust something besides your own compass.] Moses tries to hold on to his control of the situation and make sense of this experience, but it isn't working.

In the language of the spiritual journey, this was a good thing. "I'm not the right guy for the job," he tells God about five times, but God continues to talk him into going to Pharaoh's court anyway. Finally, Moses gives in. "Alright, mysterious God, whatever you are, I'll do what you want me to do," he says, although it seems impossible to him. That's faith. That's letting go. Now it's happening. But there was just one more thing; he can't help himself. He has to exert just one more effort at not surrendering. Moses is doing what we human beings do: Before I totally give in and turn into a wimp and trust this mystery, before I make this ridiculously illogical change in my life, I'm going to attempt one more moment of control.

He says to God, "Tell me your name, O Mystery of the Universe, so that I'll know what to tell the children of Israel and the court of Pharaoh when they ask who has sent me." This sounds very theological, but on a personal level for Moses, it is really an attempt to understand what has just happened. If you know someone's name in the Old Testament, then you have a relationship with them that you partly control; if you act in their name—as in, "Open up in the name of the law"—then you carry their authority. This is Moses' last shot at figuring this whole thing out with any degree of rationality.

God sees the struggle within Moses, and gives Moses the answer Moses needed in order to do the work God has called him to. God answers: "I Am." As in, "That's all you're getting from me. Now go do what I told you to do, and all further information will be given when you need to know it. I'll be with you. I'll give you what you need. I am enough. And you are enough. Now get out of here. Show's over." And the really great part is: Moses does it.

In the last four hundred years, Western Christianity has often tended to want to make everything about knowing the right answer. Even in this twenty-first century postmodern culture, many Christians have elected to hold the fort and rely on the formula—I'm saved, I'm baptized, I've accepted Jesus as Lord, my denomination is the right denomination, whatever. And that's fine. But I think the Church has missed it in some ways, because not knowing can be a greater an act of faith than knowing is. For Moses to go back to the greatest empire on earth to challenge its Pharaoh isn't smart or logical; it's just obedience to something he had experienced in his soul. Jesus told His friends to step out of the boat they were in and walk with Him on the water. Jumping out of the boat isn't about knowing—it's about *not* knowing; that's its entire purpose. If someone's religion is about deep trust and faith, then that's healthy. But to say that you're sure that you're in God's favorite club because you know the correct dogma or formula may be modern, but it's not spiritual. I promise you: Just about the time you say you've figured God out, get ready, because what you think you've figured out about God is infinitely small—and God is infinitely big.

Many, many people have used Christianity as a weapon. That's what happens when you decide that you have a monopoly on truth. It's true of a hundred other organizations and philosophies as well. Human beings always adopt a way to think or behave to have some sense of security. But to believe that your system is the only way in which God has ever spoken or worked is idolatry. And it can lead to terribly unhealthy applications of religion—the Crusades, the Inquisition, the acceptance of Nazism by the European church, anti-Semitism, the Church's complicity in the oppression of African-Americans and Native Americans. The list goes on and on.

So if you find it hard to swallow institutional religion sometimes like me, you probably don't want be part of a church that permits that kind of behavior and thinking.

After all, why not use religion? I can control it because I know the answer. And it's easier to know the answer. You don't have to be vulnerable. Everyone else is wrong; everyone else is the enemy; everyone else deserves to be punished. But that kind of self-assurance doesn't communicate any true spiritual maturity or growth. And then, people who are not necessarily sure that they know the right answer, or people like Moses who've had experiences of God that they can't explain, can get really burned by the religions that insist on their own rightness.

Melanie is a woman who grew up in a happy Southern Baptist home, though the denomination isn't the real issue. It could've been an environmentalist home, a Republican home, a Hispanic home, a Greek home, a Presbyterian home, or an agnostic home. Any identity or philosophy, when in the hands of someone who swings it around like a bat, or uses it to hold people down, has the potential to harm everyone else. And this home turned out to be that kind of system.

Melanie's father was the pastor of their church. He was adamant that their religious beliefs were the only ones that were valid, and felt that people who didn't believe in Jesus exactly in the same way he did were going straight to hell. He dragged his family out every Saturday to go door-to-door, speaking to people about Jesus and accepting Him as Lord And Savior. They went on mission trips to help the poor. They collected cans for the church's building fund. They had Bible study time as a family every night, as well as going to church three times a week.

Melanie's father also beat the crap out of her regularly, going crazy and attacking her and her brother and sister with a belt or a hairbrush. Just because he felt like it. It was the family's little secret. Nobody said anything because the rule said that God has made the man the head of the household, and everyone else is to submit. Dad would cry afterward and ask for forgiveness.

Melanie got out of there when she was eighteen and never looked back. But, of course she looked back many times a day, feeling the wounds in her back and neck and feet and heart. She couldn't allow herself to open up to the possibility of ever being married, ever opening up to anyone in any sort of vulnerable or committed relationship, and especially of ever going back to church. So she ran. She happened to pick sex, drugs, and rock and roll as her coping devices, but there are lots of others—anything to get away from what burned you. Denial works—"Oh, that never really happened," or, "You're blowing it out of proportion. It wasn't so bad!" Or there's always more and more consuming and buying. Anger can also silence the voices. Replacing one repressive way of life with another. Or just repeating the problem by recreating it in your own life—like, beating up the ones you love, or running to a new, stricter religion, or becoming a workaholic. Melanie chose drugs and alcohol. It's an easy mistake; any one of us could've made it. Her real issue wasn't alcohol anyway; alcohol was just a tool that was available.

She married young, had three babies, fought with her husband, and drank and smoked more and more and more. Got a job as a computer systems analyst for a nice big company and looked good to everyone out there. But finally, she and her husband couldn't live together anymore, so they split, and he left her with the children. She was so angry all the time that she didn't even see that she was destroying herself. And why wouldn't she? Her childhood had been a nightmare, there weren't any people she could trust, and God was a raging beast in the sky waiting to burn her up for her sins.

But a few years later, as happens with lots of alcoholics, Melanie hit bottom, looked around, felt somewhere inside that she wanted to live rather than die, and began going to A.A. meetings. She got better. She began to give herself some room. She met a nice guy, also in recovery, which is the term twelve-step participants use for the process of learning not only to be sober but, more, how to be a whole person. They got married. Melanie started going to a therapist once a week. She's been going for eight years now, and she's more and more sane and sober all the time. She's still getting healed.

God, however, was still an unknowable, unapproachable, unloving abstraction, a fire below her and a gigantic weight hanging over her. Melanie has told me that the worst part of A.A. was the first step: giving up control of one's life to a higher power. For her, the higher power was the tyrannical God who was the spiritual equivalent of her flawed, abusive father. But somehow, over months and months with other A.A. members who helped her, she did it. She practiced the steps. She began to surrender. It felt like failure at first, like giving in to that bastard God. But God turned out to be different than she'd thought.

Some friends happened to mention that they went to a church that didn't talk about God being about judgment, but emphasized grace and forgiveness and healing. They invited her to come sometime if she ever felt like it. After months and months of thinking about it, she did, although it was all she could take to put one butt cheek on the end of the highest pew in the very back of the auditorium. She's still going, albeit a little reluctantly. And now, years later, She's starting to begin to maybe—possibly—believe that there really are such things as love and grace.

Melanie doesn't buy most conventional Christian doctrine, even though she attends a Christian church. Doctrine is of no interest to her. She has something else; she has faith. She told me recently, "I don't know what I believe anymore in terms of religion. But I know there is a God. Does that mean I'm okay? Or am I doomed to hell?" I asked her what she thought. She said she doesn't know, but that she's just going to keep going to church and raising her children and working to keep her sobriety and serenity. I told her she knows God *intimately*.

I find Melanie to be one of the most courageous people I know. She's amazing. She doesn't know the intellectual answers anymore—doesn't care about the answers—but just cares about following her heart and the voice of God as she understands God, literally a day at a time, even an hour at a time. She knows something that isn't theology or doctrine. She knows something more important than that.

She has a "we'll see" mind. The "we'll see" mind is courageous. It dares to say, "I don't know the answer. The answers of previous generations and ways of knowing what is true don't fit me, and now I'm ready simply to see what happens, find out who I am and where to go from here."

At The Bridge, Kelly is being transformed. Slowly, with lots of backward steps as well as forward ones, she is learning that it's possible to trust something. It required that she stop running so fast. Slow down. Breathe. Feel something. That's not passive; it's hard work, not for wimps.

I respect the people at The Bridge. They amaze me. Their pastor, Ken, is a guy with a shaved head and tattoos and funky clothes on. He didn't start out that way; he was a normal pastor in the suburbs. But something in his heart was telling him that God wanted out of that box. He went to Portland and helped to start this downtown gathering of people. Ken has told me that they don't condemn people at The Bridge. The teens and young adults who show up are already so terrified and wounded, how can you condemn them any further? Why would you want to? The church is full of chain smokers, punks, homosexuals, substance abusers, and the freaks nobody else wants. Ken doesn't turn anyone away, even the ones doing drugs or having irresponsible sex. "We don't judge them; we welcome them," he says. "In time, when they realize we're not going to tell them they're going to hell if they don't stop drinking or whatever it is they're into, and they see that God is doing great things for people, they may decide to stop drinking or doping. But that's not a condition for people being accepted by God. It's the opposite. The example of Jesus is that God wants people as they are. Then it's up to God to change people. All I can do is offer love to them. So I just hold their hands or listen to their stories and tell them mine. Sometimes they open up and get better. But I can't heal anybody; that's God's job." He adds, "I certainly can't do anything for anyone by being the pastor, or knowing some set response to their lives. I'm just there to love them with God's love."

Melanie is getting healed all the time because she can trust something, but not something that tells her to trust it before it is willing to encounter her. She is learning to trust as she encounters what loves her and what she believes she can love in return. So is Kelly.

I am finding that the more I let go of my own control of my agenda, my schedule, my life, my answers, my opinions, the more free I become. I can actually just breathe and trust that there is something or someone that will be with me.

This lets me be wild. God is wild; I am absolutely convinced of that. God is madly uncontained. In response to God's madness, we've tried to tame God, we've decided how much we want God around, and we've told the God of the universe to stay within that small space—history, theology, philosophy, stained glass, art, mythology, morality, blah blah blah. But whatever could have created the physical world around us must be amazing and diverse and odd and wonderful and terrible all at once. Not stained glass. Not tidy.

Walk through a forest or watch animals a while. Look under a microscope. Watch human beings. Listen to your heart. Or *really* read the Bible. Nothing you notice will behave itself. A lot of what you see won't be pretty, wouldn't make it to a minivan commercial on television. But it will be real, and therefore sacred and beautiful.

Jesus is wild, amazing, unpredictable. He touches people He shouldn't; He weeps with whores and dances with poor people. He heals what is broken. And He doesn't talk an awful lot about doctrine. Instead, He talks a lot about faith—the kind that means you step out into the unknown. You are willing to try to love, to give up some of your power, to let go of control. To trust something. To even begin to believe down in your guts somewhere what God seems to be saying over and over: It's your willingness to trust something that makes you well. You are enough. It is enough.

How did Jesus get through His temptation experience, His being rejected by everyone, His crucifixion? He had a sense, deep down, that He was not alone. How did Martin Luther King, Jr., or Gandhi, or Sojourner Truth, or the painter Georgia O'Keeffe, or any of the countless unnamed people who've done amazing things, do what they did? Not on their own. They let go. They surfed. They trusted something and kept going.

In the U2 song, "Walk On," Bono sings about letting go.

> All that you fashion
> All that you make
> All that you build
> And all that you break
> All that you measure
> All that you steal
> All this you can leave behind [6]

At the end of their concerts in the second half of their Elevation tour in 2001/2002, Bono and The Edge would lead the crowd in singing "Walk On," and then add on top of it a repeated "Halle, halle, hallelujah," a celebration of the freedom that comes when you leave it all behind and just trust that there's something worth leaving it behind for. Jesus said, "None of you can be my followers if you don't give up all you possess." He doesn't mean it as an impossible and cruel demand, although that's how we take it. He means it as a gift. Give up all you possess, all you're carrying around. Let it go.

Hallelujah.

6 U2, Bono and The Edge, lyrics, "Walk On," *All That You Can't Leave Behind*, PolyGram International Music Publishing B. V.; c2000 Universal International Music B. V., Interscope Records 3145246532.

NEW WOUND, NEW NAME

CHAPTER_ **6**

In one very old story, there are twin boys, and when the second of the twins is born, he comes out of the womb holding on to his older brother's heel. His parents name him Jacob, which means "the one who grabs." It's also a name that can mean "the one who tricks," or "the one who steals." Not a great name. But, it seems to me, it's a name that fits our culture; we grab everything—food, cars, entertainment, vacations, clothes, security, doctrine, politics, whatever. Of course, don't feel bad; this story is thousands of years old, so we're not the first human beings to have this tendency.

Jacob is the mama's boy of the two sons. Esau, in contrast to wiry little Jacob, is a big, hairy hunter—and his father's favorite. Isaac, the boys' father and the patriarch of the tribe, grows to be an old, nearly blind man, and when he knows he's approaching death, he announces that it's time for the official ceremony in which he'll pass the blessing of the family down to Esau. Isaac asks Esau to go out on a hunting trip and catch him something good, and then return and prepare his favorite meal for the ceremony. Rebekah, the mother, decides that this is Jacob's chance. She encourages him to trick Isaac into giving Jacob the blessing reserved for the firstborn son. This blessing belongs to Esau of course and not Jacob, but, after all, Jacob is "the one who grabs."

Mama and Jacob hurry around while Esau's gone and prepare Isaac's meal, then Jacob puts Esau's robe on and ties goatskins on his arms and neck. He goes into Isaac's tent, carrying the food, saying, "O Great Isaac, Father of the Nation, Your Son has returned with this meal to honor you on this sacred day." Isaac asks who he thinks is Esau to come and kneel before him. Wondering if something is wrong, he touches the skins on Jacob's arms, breathes in the smell of Esau's robe, and is satisfied.

Isaac eats the big meal, and when he's feasted and celebrated, he brings Jacob to stand in front of him and passes his family's blessing on to Jacob. And "the one who grabs," grabs it. Welcome to America, where we are given the right to grab life, liberty, and the pursuit of happiness. If you can earn it, that's good; if you have to take it from the native people who were here already, or plan a killer business strategy so you can leverage it from someone else's company, or work seventy hours a week so you can buy it at the mall, that's okay too.

Esau comes in moments later with the meal he's prepared, and Isaac realizes what's happened. In a terrible scene, he tells Esau that the blessing's been passed along already, and that now he has none to give. That seems strange to us today, but carefully structured rules were what held every-thing together in tribal cultures. The world outside the family compound was hostile, literally—they were living in the desert with no one around for miles except rival tribes. The hierarchy that told everyone where

they belonged in the tribe was the method they used to keep power central-
ized and the tribe strong. Jacob and his mother just figured out how to
trick that system. We call it good ol' American ingenuity.

Esau vows to get revenge, so their mother talks Isaac into sending Jacob
far away, to find a suitable wife. Rather than face what he's done and be
reconciled with Esau, Jacob runs away from home. He travels across the
desert, and has a vision from God, a dream in which he sees angels
climbing up and down a ladder. He takes this as a sign that God is with
him, and proceeds.

Jacob's alone and hurt, which can be good for his spiritual journey.
However, he's not broken enough yet to be truly healed. He travels
not into the desert but across it. He's got things to accomplish. He gets out
of there as quick as he can. So far, this guy is the twentieth century action-
adventure hero of ancient Israel.

He meets his mother's family and plans are made for him to marry one
of his distant cousins, Rachel. Jacob works for Rachel's father, Laban, for
seven years, waiting to marry her. But in an ironic twist, Rachel's father,
Laban, tricks Jacob into marrying Rachel's older sister, Leah—and then
lets Jacob marry Rachel, but the price for marrying her is that Jacob has to
work another seven years. The trickster gets tricked.

So Jacob gets even. Along the way, Jacob and his wives and their servant
girls end up producing twelve sons and a daughter between them. This is
prosperity—a large tribe was the goal, sort of like a big house with a big
garage, lots of cars, a boat, a big flat-screen television, and a great portfolio.
Jacob builds up his and Laban's flocks, and they both become rich men.
But Jacob works out an agreement with Laban to separate their flocks

based on their coloring. Jacob, of course, sets up the process so that he'll end up with the bigger herds. After a while, Laban and his sons realize what Jacob's been doing, and vow to get revenge, just as Esau did a generation earlier. So, just as before, Jacob runs away, out across the desert.

However, this time, the place he realizes he will be headed is back to his father's home. But now it's Esau's home. This is terrifying. Esau is surely going to come at him with an army. In a tribal culture, a crime against your family is an offense that will get you killed; think about the Corleones in *The Godfather* movie series, or the Sopranos on HBO, or hillbillies having a feud.

But Jacob decides that he has nowhere else to go. It's time to go home. This is where he begins to grow up, finally. This is going to mean that it's possible for him to begin to be a healed person. This won't be about "grabbing" anything; it will be about letting go.

And he has to go back into that same desert. That's important. He didn't go far enough down spiritually the first time he came through; yes, he was traveling into the desert, but not toward something. The journey into the desert is not a journey away from; it's a journey into. It's purposeful. It's about surrender. It's not about building your fortune; it's about finding something that will last much longer. The Buddhists talk about detachment from the things that keep you from where your soul belongs. But just to run past your stuff and say you're letting go isn't detachment.

As Jacob heads out, after reaching an agreement with Laban before he leaves, Jacob has another dream. In this dream, an army of angels from God appears before him. He takes this dream as a good sign as well. He's right, although not for the reason he or we would naturally assume. His first dream was of angels going up and down a ladder to heaven—God telling him there's a larger, spiritual dimension to his life than simply making it across the desert and amassing a big family and riches. The dream said, *Jacob, if you are smart enough to acknowledge this larger sense of who you are, God will be present with you in your journey, bringing you what you need.* He sort of understood. In this second dream, the angels have come down to stand with him. He thinks an army of angels is coming to fight on his side. I think it means more than that. I think it means that he's being fortified for the battle he's about to undergo spiritually and emotionally. He's finally doing the work.

And there's still one more angel to come.

Jacob and his family and servants and herds and slaves all cross the desert. When they are close to the lands which now belong to his brother, Esau—home doesn't belong to Jacob anymore; he's denied who he was—Jacob tries to figure out how to make things turn out all right.

This is not a sentimental made-for-TV movie in which, no matter where you go, you can always come back home and all will be well. We know life isn't that simple. And we're a very mobile culture; you go to college and then head out to make your fortune, leave your tribe, and make your way in a far country. Most adults I know joke about the joys of going back home to their relatives' houses for holidays—"Oh well, wish me luck; I'm off to Dysfunction Junction" or "Well, back to the old home place. I'm excited. I haven't visited the 1970's lately." It's odd; you go back home, but it's not home anymore. It hasn't changed, but you have. And yet, there is a need in our souls to return home, even if that doesn't mean physically returning. In fact, it's a process that's probably better done without returning to the house or apartment you grew up in. It's soul work, figuring out what you left behind but are still carrying around. But, unlike television, this is real, and it's hard.

Jacob wants to soften this process as much as possible; after all, facing who you are and what you've done can be dangerous, especially if you're the one who grabs. He sends a servant to Esau's house with a promise of gifts and livestock. The messenger comes back and tells Jacob that Esau is coming with four hundred men. Jacob knows he can't win a battle against an army. So he says a prayer, divides up his livestock, treasures, servants, children and wives, and sends the least precious things and people ahead to face Esau. He then sends the more precious things—his four wives and his many children—across a narrow place in a river separating where he came from and where Esau lives, to have them wait until morning, when they'll all go together to face Esau and his army.

Jacob waits back on the other side of the river. A river in a myth or tribal story is a symbol of a character's passage from one part of his or her journey to the next phase of the journey. A lesson. A loss. A victory. A threshold between two rooms in one's life. Then, the text says, simply, "So Jacob was left alone." This is a first. Nobody to bargain with, no weapons. No possessions or riches. Nowhere to go. No fortune to go and build. He's given it all up; for all he knows, everything he owns is already in the hands of his enemy.

Now we can get down to it. In the morning, it will be time for Jacob to meet what he's been running from for twenty years. He's finally here. There's no trick that will keep this confrontation from happening. And while Jacob thinks it's Esau that he's having to face, it's not. The entire verse says, "So Jacob was left alone, and a man wrestled with him till daybreak."

The text doesn't say who the man is; it simply calls him "the man." Spiritually and emotionally speaking, the man is Jacob himself, his fears, and his ambitions. This is a symbol of spiritual struggle. But this isn't one of the many times in Jacob's life when he was trying to get something by climbing over someone else. This is Jacob simply wrestling deep inside with who he really is and who he will become. Jacob has finally come to the end of himself, and he has the opportunity to end his lifelong pattern of avoiding responsibility. And so this is also a story about meeting and wrestling with God, who has been waiting all this time to meet us, as soon as we can slow down enough to pay attention.

Most of us never really struggle with our darkest selves, the man or woman in the dark, the thing that is with us when we are alone and all of our defenses have been sent ahead. We decide to kill what scares us or threatens us—just to get rid of it. Native Americans. The wilderness. Blacks, Mexicans, the rich, the poor, gays, Democrats, Republicans, Christians, nonbelievers—you pick yours. At the end of every horror movie or fairy tale, the monster in the dark has to die; that's our way of telling ourselves our own darkness isn't going to stay around. But in the movies, you get rid of Jason or whoever, not with wisdom or surrender, but with violence. This is a deeply tribal solution. Kill the wicked witch, or Frankenstein's monster, or the dragon. Radical Muslims. Abortion clinics. Fundamentalists. Whatever. Destroy what lurks out there. That seems the logical thing to do: Blow it up. But in a way, blowing up the enemy is a way of giving up rather than wrestling. Wrestling is about encounter and understanding. That's much harder. So we run. We deny.

And we're part of a culture that encourages running rather than wrestling. We sedate ourselves and our feelings—strangely, the good as well as the bad—with chemicals, food, rage, work, sex, whatever. We can actually avoid the shadow forever. But to be a whole person, eventually it becomes time to stop running, and face what's been kept in hiding. The ones who face their Shadows can become great warriors, spiritual guides, powerful healers. They can make amazing moms, co-workers, musicians, and teachers. They can be truly compassionate. The desert is the place where we finally head out so far that there's no way to find our way back before we give up all we brought with us and wrestle with what's inside. And we get stronger.

The story says that Jacob and the man wrestle all night. This is life and death stuff, what the classical Christian mystic tradition calls The Dark Night of the Soul. Jacob the grabber holds on tight. He's made a difficult journey, and his road has been his teacher; now he's finally ready to go all the way into the darkness of his hidden self. All of his sadness, all of his loss, all of the grief he was never able to feel for the loss of his father—he was gone from home when Isaac died—can come swimming up from the deep places.

The man—we still haven't been told whether this is an angel, or a warrior, or what—realizes that he's not going to be able to subdue Jacob. The story says that the man knocks Jacob's hip out of joint in order to escape. This is what the mythic tradition calls the "sacred wound." King Arthur sails away with one. The resurrected Jesus bears the marks of His crucifixion. Women's bodies and hearts are changed forever after the wounding trauma of giving birth. God commands the men of ancient Israel to carry circumcision on their bodies, a ritual scarring, as a sign of their being part of a separate tribe. Luke Skywalker loses a hand. Boys and girls in tribal cultures have scars on their faces from initiation ceremonies. These wounds are the remnants of our baptisms and our deaths and rebirths. You live through the dying process, but you're never the same. You have a story to tell. You know what it is to feel pain. Gandalf the Grey in *The Lord of the Rings* falls to his death in the depths of the Earth—but returns, reborn, as Gandalf the White, with greater wisdom and power than he could ever have had before.

But the modern adult doesn't want to be wounded. You take a pill for every little ailment. Commercials promise that there is never any reason to feel pain or even to have an unmet need. The ideal body shows no scars of any kind; it's perfect and young. All is well. "How are you today?" "Fine."

But not to be allowed to carry the marks and scars of the struggles you've had is to deny that you've ever struggled with anything you couldn't defeat—which is spiritually deadening and sick. You can't always be the football team that's undefeated. Where's the lesson in that? Yet that's what we're taught. A famous football coach says to his players, "Winning isn't everything; it's the only thing," and we all write it down on our "You Can Be A Success Today" calendar. But Jesus never pushes us to win; He encourages us to die. That's where victory and wholeness are. [But then, Jesus would make a terrible football coach. He'd want to equip the team members with servant's hearts, compassion, and courage in facing hypocrisy. They'd run some plays, then take a break, laugh, dance, spread out a big meal in the middle of the field and invite everybody. They'd sit and cry with the opposing player who's just broken up with his girlfriend. And they'd tell the overbearing coach that if he doesn't quit telling everyone they have to win, he should shove it and get lost.]

The story says Jacob walks with a limp from then on after his wrestling match. This is a good thing. He's not just the rich man anymore; he's the rich man who knows what it is to suffer and survive. If he had stayed the rich man with flocks and a tribe and riches in a faraway land, it would have been fun, but he would have simply ended up as a rich man with an empire. Now he's the wounded son, brother, and husband who has learned compassion and true strength.

The mysterious man in the darkness has to get free of this strong, struggling man before the sun comes up. That's how it works for the beings that live in the dark; they aren't meant to be looked at too closely in the light. The whole point is that they are only present when we are willing to face the darkness, to be silent, to be still. But then, that's why we're afraid of the dark; those things are out there. In here. Somebody turn the television on. So the man says to Jacob, "You've got to let me go before the new day comes."

Jacob realizes something. In being willing to wrestle with the man in the darkness, he is becoming healed. The sun is about to come up. He made it. A new day is about to begin for him. So he says, "I'll let you go if you give me a blessing." This is not a blessing that makes everything go your way, or gives you property or a family inheritance or good luck. This is different from the blessing that belonged to Esau, that Jacob tricked Isaac into giving to him instead, the blessing that Jacob stole. This is the healing of the sacred wound. This is something that doesn't belong to Esau or anyone else. Finally, Jacob is ready for the real blessing that he was hungry for all along. The blessing that belongs to him.

The man asks him his name. This is part of the process of growing up and becoming a mature human being. You have to accept who you are in order to grow further. In ancient stories, as in the example of Moses wanting to know the name of God, a character's name is in some ways the definition of that character. This is a direct question: Who are you? What kind of life have you led? What defines you? And are you willing to face up to what your life is about? If you're not, you can't receive the blessing that God has for you. And there is a part of you right now [whether you're away from home or still in it, starting a career or avoiding one, with a family or alone] that knows the answer to the question, "What is your name?" The trick is getting into the dark enough and wrestling long enough that you can answer yourself and God honestly.

Jacob answers honestly. That's also a first. He doesn't flinch. He doesn't say, "I'm the famous head of a huge tribe" or "I'm the one who carries the inheritance of the great chieftain Isaac"—he just answers, "I'm the one who grabs and steals." That is his entire identity. Maybe it's all he ever thinks he'll be.

But the man who wrestles says, "You're going to have a new name." In Alcoholics Anonymous, the requirement is that you stand up when it's time to be welcomed or time to speak, and say who you are: "I'm Rick, and I'm an alcoholic." You've told the truth about yourself. In the language of the Church, you've confessed—an act so holy and important that it has been considered a basic part of being "saved." And, with that kind of honesty in God's presence, there is forgiveness, pardon, healing. You are given a new identity. You're set free.

The man says to Jacob, "Here is your blessing. Your new name is Israel, the one who wrestles with God, because you have been wrestling with God, and you've made it through."

Each of us, all along, is both running from God and wrestling with God. Each of us, in every phase of our lives, is given the opportunity to face who we are and what we've chosen, or to deny who we are and keep grabbing. I'm usually somewhere in the middle.

The man says to Jacob, Now you've finally quit running, you've held on, you've prevailed, and you've come home. You are becoming a whole human being. That's your blessing.

Jacob, amazed, asks, "What is your name?" It's natural. We want to make sense of what's just happened. But, as in the Moses story, mystery isn't that easily categorized. The man replies, "Why do you want to know my name?" It's not about me; it's about you, the one who wrestles with God. I'll be around. Don't be afraid. Look how far you've come.

And then the man in the darkness disappears. The night is over. The earth turns and the sun appears. It's time to go and face the music and find out what to do with what you've become so far. This is definitely not something our culture wants—no culture has ever wanted this. No person wants this. That's why we run.

But it's the key to spiritual healing. Which is ironic, because we avoid facing who we are so that we'll stay happy, when real wholeness comes from facing it. So we say, "It wasn't me! I didn't do it! It was my parents! I think I'll sue someone!" It almost never happens that a public figure comes forward and talks about being wounded, or broken, or stupid, although with more and more acceptance of twelve-step programs as a healthy way to deal with what we've chosen, there are more people who are willing to be honest. We have heard people say, "I have cancer," or, "I'm an alcoholic and I'm going to go into recovery. I hope you'll get in touch with who you are and begin healing." I wish there were a good way to say, "I'm a sex addict, like the rest of this culture; I'm a success addict, like the rest of this culture. I'm a rage-aholic. I can't stop trying to win all the time. I have to be perfect. I love money. And I'm going to go into recovery. I hope you'll get in touch with who you are and begin healing."

The odd thing is, another way to avoid facing the consequences of what you've chosen is to take on guilt that's not yours. *I am the chief of sinners,* the apostle Paul writes in a moment of self-importance. Saying that you're scum, that you're the most sinful person who ever lived makes you special—and it works nicely because that means you don't have to be in touch with what you actually have chosen and what that means.

Jacob—who is now Israel—does an amazing thing. Israel doesn't deny who he is and what he's done. Instead, he crosses the stream, joins his family, and walks out in front of them all to meet his brother's army and his brother at the head.

He limps across the plain, carrying his wound and his new name, to confess who he is and who he has been, and to return to a home that is and isn't his anymore. He doesn't have to live there or run from it. He is free.

The Fire and Letting Go

The kinds of initiation and transformation that Jacob undergoes are more than what's symbolized in water baptism, more than a death and rebirth. This kind of life requires a willingness to continue to wrestle. John Who Baptized says of Jesus, "The one who is coming after I'm here won't baptize with water; He will baptize with the Spirit of God, and with fire." To continue to be refined, to struggle, to confess again and again, to return again and again, is a way of living that is alive and threatening. It's like being bathed in fire, over and over.

The Jesus that I encounter in the gospels is not tidy. He isn't safe. He isn't a three-point sermon; He's more like an unpredictable series of explosions going off. He's a threat to almost everything—except those who are broken, lost, and open. Those whose houses have been picked up by tornados and flung across the sky. Those who have ended up in the desert. Jesus went to the desert. He knows what it is. He has His sacred wounds.

Because of this, Jesus is completely free. He isn't interested in anyone's rules or ideas. He is immoral in the very best sense of the word; the morals and conventional wisdom of the culture are his enemies. Jesus' job is to set people free, as He says in His first sermon in his home church, quoting a poem written a few hundred years earlier by an Israelite prophet:

> The spirit of the Lord has come into me.
> It has chosen me to give the poor some good news.
> It has sent me to go tell prisoners that they are to be set free,
> And I am to make the blind see again,
> And I am to give oppressed people relief.
> I have been chosen to tell everyone that the time is here
> when all debts are cancelled and all sins forgiven.
> God approves of you. You are free.[7]

Radical stuff. Culture-shattering. If Jesus' plans come true, no institution that is based on rules and regulations can remain standing. And the strange thing is that this statement by Jesus about His central purpose is supposedly one of the foundations of Christian theology and practice, but most churches in the West accomplish the exact opposite of this mission statement of Jesus'. But Jesus is undeterred.

For Jesus, to be modern is a sin—in the sense that Jesus repeatedly reacts against there being one answer. Jesus went to church and studied the Scriptures like a good boy, but He also threw furniture around in the church when He saw that what the Church really wanted was not to be an

7 Jesus, in Luke 4:17-19, quoting Isaiah 6

instrument of God's heart, but to maintain its hold on its own power. I mean, He literally threw furniture and beat people in the church office and the capitol building with a whip.

Jesus broke every rule and moral code He could find. He broke rules about how you had to prepare for meals, where to sit at a formal dinner, how to speak respectfully to those who were supposed to be honored, and how to respond to political power. He loved whores and their pimps; the dope-dealers and the bikers; the jocks and the stoners; the ex-cons and the manual laborers. He was one of them, one of the poorest of the poor, an outsider from birth. He loved to drink and laugh and dance. He also would weep wildly when His heart was broken. He believed that there are some things worth standing up for. He also believed passionately that there are some things worth standing up against, which for Him was anything having to do with religion's monopoly on truth, and its refusal to include people who didn't possess the right answer or act the right way.

The caretakers of the institutions demanded that the rules Jesus broke were non-negotiable. He'd respond that God was fed up with them and that God was going to throw them out like trash into a burning garbage heap outside of town, which was named Gehenna, which is translated, hell. *Go to hell, religious people,* Jesus said.

Jesus refused to be categorized. Every denomination and political party wanted Him to join their cause, and He refused. He knew that God is bigger than any man-made thing, any one way of seeing. He did not behave. He committed every kind of blasphemy. And yet, He believed that the ultimate blasphemy was to say you know the right answer—which in the first century was the equivalent of the modern mind of the twentieth century.

Jesus said repeatedly that there is no one right answer. There are many answers. "I have flocks you don't know anything about," He told His followers. Basically, "You're not the center of the universe. Get over yourselves." The leaders of the institutional church would tell Him that He was wrong to welcome and embrace people who hadn't been to Bible study, or said the correct creeds, or whatever. Jesus would tell the leaders to shut up and leave God's people alone. The leaders within His own movement came to Him at one point and complained, "There are other churches out there that are using your name to heal people! Give us the okay to make them stop!" What they were saying was, "That's not right! It's not fair! They don't belong to our club! They can't possibly be right! We're the only ones who are right!" Jesus' response to them was: "Leave them alone. They're not against us, so they're for us." That is, "You're not the only ones with a connection to God. Leave other people alone. Lots of others besides you will be doing what my Father wants for the people of the world."

Jesus included everybody. He healed everybody. He forgave everybody. He accepted everybody. He threw grace and wholeness around randomly, like a farmer sewing seeds in a field, hoping they'll take root. The leaders of the big denominations would insist that He stop celebrating so much. Jesus would tell them that God's love transforms everything into one big banquet—and that they wouldn't be allowed inside if they didn't stop being so self-righteous. They decided that they had to shut Him up somehow, which would eventually mean that He'd have to be executed. He expected that. So He promised them: "God's love is so powerful, you can shut me up for a day or two, but I can't be contained. I am a sign of God's grace. God is wild. You can't keep me in a box or a tomb or a religion or whatever. God's love will break the door down." That's what Jesus' resurrection is about: God's love breaking out of the box. It's too bad religion keeps trying to put Him back in.

One of the images of the Spirit of God used in the middle ages in northern
Europe is the wild goose—it flies around wherever it wants to and lands
where it will. You don't hold onto safe answers when you know the Spirit;
you give them away and just fly. You don't know where you're going next;
Jesus just says, "Follow me." In order to follow something that wild and
free, someone that liberating and empowering, you're going to have to let
some things go. Just as was true with entering the desert, it becomes time
to let go of our weapons and just walk in. But following the Spirit doesn't
lead you to become something less than you are; you become something
more. You are free to grow larger and larger, stronger and more courageous,
because you're free to let everything go.

Jesus' temptations were about letting go of the desires He had to be powerful and important. He let those desires drop by the side of the road He
was walking, and then traveled easier and faster. That's why Jesus gave to
His followers this gift: "Anyone who wants to be one of my followers
should pick up a cross and follow me"—pick up an instrument of execu-
tion, and when you face the death of whatever needs to go, you'll be
ready to see the presence of God in your everyday life. You think that if you
start letting go, the thing that is going to die is you. But it's not. It's just
stuff.

This is how Jesus can show love for His own executioners. The stories say
that as He was dying on His cross, He prayed that God would forgive
them—as Jesus was already forgiving them. He had let go of everything.
And so His work was, as He said on the cross, finished.

If you are able to let go of everything that isn't necessary because you really
don't need anything, then suddenly, as Richard Rohr says, everything
belongs. All things become sacred because you accept that everything you

experience is part of your journey. You don't have to hold onto anything or reject anything. All of your hates and loves, grudges and fears, joyous moments and celebrations—they're all sacred. All your wounds are sacred. All people are sacred, just as they are, already. You don't have to like everybody, but that's not the point. And so you're free to see it, decide if you want to carry it any longer, and keep traveling.

In one sense, Jesus' final assessment of His ministry—"It is finished!"—means, "It is alright. It is good. It is very good." How can someone who is facing death feel this? Because, as God says of the new creation He's spoken into being in the book of Genesis, whatever God does "is very good." This seems so contradictory to what Christians are taught. Yet it's so clearly what Jesus was all about—and it's the only God that the "we'll see" mind is ultimately really interested in. It's the God who is big enough to welcome every question and every experience.

The American poet Walt Whitman said, "Do I contradict myself? Very well then, I contradict myself. I am vast. I contain multitudes." Surely God is vast enough to contain multitudes of things that seem to us to be incompatible, but make perfectly good sense to God. "Oh, by the way, disciples—the laws of physics? We're going to throw those out today. Today we're walking on water." *That's impossible!* "Oh? Sorry—I just did it." Jesus refuses to see Himself as an answer-giver. One scholar says that Jesus is asked 183 questions in the gospels, and answers three. How not modern of Him.

God isn't an answer-giver either—read the Old Testament. God is stubbornly contradictory and complex. God is mystery. The night of His arrest, just before the soldiers are coming to arrest, torture, and execute Him, Jesus begs his Father to come up with another plan.

What He hears from God is silence. And Jesus understands. So, accepting this deep within, He says, "Alright. This is what you and I have decided together to do. It's not the answer I want, but it's what has to happen." It's no surprise; this willingness to live without external surety is Jesus' consistent way of living and teaching. He lets go—and gets everything he ever wanted.

Freedom is terrifying. No one really wants to go to the desert and be stripped. No one wants to be that naked. No one wants to let go of everything. So we construct philosophies, answers, and doctrines that give us security and clarity. It can be very genuine to want a "1 Answer" God—one answer for all things.

But ultimately the "we'll see" mind can't be satisfied with one answer. Our experience is just too complex and rich. We embrace it, all of what it is, all of who we are. Then we are able to let go. And so we are free. Alanis Morissette sings in her song "Thank You":

The moment I let go of it
Was the moment I got more than I could handle
The moment I jumped off of it
Was the moment when I touched down.[8]

Jesus says that all we need is faith the size of a mustard seed, the size of a fat grain of pepper, the size of a grain of sand. Set down all those trunk loads of answers, and just walk. This makes sense to the "we'll see" mind. In the twenty-first century mind, all are welcome. For the children born during and after the 1970s, there aren't really any significant reasons to categorize people according to race, gender, sexuality, history, age, philosophy, denomination, or politics. I see people just hanging out

[8] Alanis Morissette, lyrics, "Thank U," *Supposed Former Infatuation Junkie*, ©1998 Maverick Recording Company, 9-47094-2.

together all the time. Postmoderns seek out people who are different from them. So the welcoming Jesus is a twenty-first century God worth knowing.

If You Aren't There

Spirit-space, the way of life that is about not knowing, is where there is room for something to happen that's more than achieving my to-do list. I'm not saying that you need to go to church so you can find something worth living for; I'd personally rather spend a day walking in the hills behind my neighborhood than spend a few hours at most churches. But that's my point. Walking in the hills, or listening to my son tell me about his latest school project, or talking to a good friend, or being silent and still, are all activities that we think of as sort of useless, and yet which create space. That space doesn't exist if the television is on or I'm frustrated about someone getting in front of me in traffic.

Poet Angelus Silesius writes, *God, whose love and joy are present everywhere/Can't come and visit you unless you aren't there.* This is difficult. Of course I'll be here; where else would I be? But the issue is, all the stuff that you hold onto is what keeps God from visiting—because you're not even where you are anyway. Your brain and soul are far from your body. You've pushed them away.

Spirit-space is about not knowing, getting out of the way. It's about silence. It's about surrender. When I was an English teacher, I used to reassure students that we weren't going to dissect the poems we were looking at; we'd try to let them live. To dissect something is to kill it. But of course, there was always a part of some of us, me included, which wanted to know the answer that would be on the test. So it's a struggle. *I want to enjoy the spirit of Christmas, but I've also got to put up the stupid Christmas lights, so just hold on, Jesus, I'll get to you shortly. Thanks for stopping by, though.*

Poet Natalie Goldberg says that when you're writing your own poem or story, if something that occurs to you seems particularly grisly or unpleasant, you should write about that. "Go for the jugular," she says. That's where the truth is.

Robert Bly, a writer who grew up on a Minnesota farm, had an alcoholic father and a strict church upbringing. He says that it was twenty years after he left home before he could even begin to have an honest thought or feeling. He began to come back to life by returning to Minnesota and sitting for hours in silence, waiting for an honest thought to come. Some of them did, finally, and his truest poems were born.

Your life is a story, a poem, or a song. It's a journey. Not to tell the truth means you miss it. Maybe you build something that has lovely craft and structure, but if it's not about the soul—which is contradictory, messy, terrible, beautiful—then it's not alive. It's not the truth. Or, as the Christian tradition says, it's not the Gospel.

At The Bridge in Portland, grace is messy. The community there is not tidy. To an outsider, the lack of structure doesn't seem to make sense. And yet it works. Kim, one of the women who leads Bible studies for the young adults, told me that what has helped her healing process is that the pastor, Ken, has "modeled his vulnerability for me." Ken is broken, too, just like everybody else there. That's the truth. And that's where healing comes from.

In the life that God is part of, what Jesus calls the Kingdom of God, everyone is in the doctor's office, everyone is sick, everyone is being healed. And so everyone belongs. That's why Jesus can invite everyone to the cross. That's where you get healed from being naked, wounded, bloody, and dying to becoming a new thing. That doesn't happen when you're standing solidly on the ground; it happens when you're hanging in the air, in between things. That's spirit space. Entering that space is the truest purpose of prayer. I'm not talking about prayers—I'm talking about prayer, the means by which, when we are willing to enter spirit space, we hear what the Spirit is doing, breathing, singing, saying, being. Something we mumble in church or before we eat isn't what I'm talking about. Something the preacher says before a session of Congress isn't it either. Prayer is not knowing—and just going into that place. It can be by the side of a river, or in the car, or in the middle of an embrace, or in a hospital. But let's face it: Nobody really wants that very often. That's why we keep the DVD player on.

Jacob is finally ready to enter spirit space when he's at the river and ready to stop running. But the thing that comes to wrestle with him comes from the dark, and that's why we don't want to be in prayer—because we're afraid of what's in the dark. And it's not the stuff that's out there that scares us; it's what's within us, in the Shadow, the hidden thing we were told not to acknowledge or allow. However, the soul wants to talk to the Shadow. The soul wants to be in prayer. That's where God is, waiting to talk to us, when we get out of the way. Brent, a friend of mine who is facing a terminal illness, says, "The purification process is the beginning of mysticism. It's how we begin to see God." The purification he's talking about is the letting go and surrendering that ushers us into spirit space.

At his baptism, Jesus hears the voice of God affirm Him. Yet, on the night He is arrested, when Jesus asks God to come up with another plan than

His crucifixion and death and what He hears is silence, out of that silence,

Jesus accepts in the deepest part of Himself that His death is the ultimate reconciling, healing act He can make, and embraces it. That's spirit space.

A few years ago I was talking with a friend from church whose marriage was a total wreck and who was really in a lot of pain. He was trying to figure out whether to continue to try to make his marriage work, or get out of it, or drive off somewhere for a while. Here's one of our emails:

I need you to clear something up for me. I'm struggling with what the hell I'm doing wrong for God to want me on this road.

God doesn't want you on this road. This was never God's idea. God didn't want your mother to be alcoholic, your wife to be an alcoholic and emotionally cold, or your job to be in trouble. All that stuff is just what happens to human beings.

Am I not getting something? I'm starting to believe that I'm not getting the whole picture and I don't know if that's God saying I need to wake up.

A] There is no whole picture that's a clear answer. B] God is always wanting us to wake up, but it's never because He's frustrated that we're not understanding something. God is patient. But the bad place where we don't know the answer is a place where we can get healed up if we'll be still and not try to fix it first.

Well then, am I just setting myself up for failure? Am I screwing up?

You are doing what God wants for you, for everybody, which is, to face the truth, and be real, and have courage, and find how to stand on your own even in the face of huge pain. It will suck. It will feel like failure. But everything ends up being frustrating in one way or another. So, the answer is … pray, pray, pray. Be honest about what you're feeling, but don't demand anything from God just because you're in pain. You don't want a quick answer to this; you want the real answer. The thing you are wanting isn't in whether your circumstances are going nicely. So ordering God to fix it for us is like a toddler yelling at the mom to hand over the toy the toddler is already holding. Peace is already here. It's already possible. But we have to learn to be still. And that's what sucks. You're in pain and you don't want to be still; you want to move. But the healing is in being exactly where you are.

Being where you really are means that you awaken, and you accept what is—which means that you're not running. Peter Gabriel's song "Only Us" contains these lines:

> It wasn't in the words that kept sticking in their throats
> It wasn't with the angels in their quilted coats
> These battered wings still kick up dust
> Seduced by the noise and the bright things that glisten
> I knew all the time I should shut up and listen
> And I'm finding my way home from the great escape
> ....
> The further on I go, oh the less I know
> Friend or foe, there's only us[9]

Gabriel wrote the song during a difficult time in his life, when he and his wife were going through a divorce. You can feel it. It's a song about giving up, and stopping, and just being where you are, so you can begin to heal.

9 Peter Gabriel, "Only Us," *Us*, songs published by Real World Music Ltd, Hidden Pun Music Inc., c1992 The David Geffen Company, GEFD 24473.

In that healing process, you find something worth living for. That's the tricky part.

Andy Crouch, who speaks about postmodern spiritual growth, said at a conference a couple of years ago that in every way except one, the postmodern generation is letting go of the trappings and values of their modern parents and grandparents, but the one thing nearly everyone in America, young or old, can't let go of is consumerism. We can't stop consuming, eating, buying, wearing, driving, having. It's fun. It's a way of making your entire life like watching soap operas or music videos all the time, night and day, laughing and feeling like you're as cool as they are. But ultimately, that's not the good news. It doesn't heal.

The real thing worth wrestling is larger than that. You find something that matters, something that takes you beyond your own comfort, and slowly or suddenly your life is actually worth living, deeply and profoundly. You breathe deeper, like someone out playing Ultimate Frisbee or dancing or slowing down. You're awake. And you're wrestling in the best sense. It's like feeling ready to start playing racquetball with someone who plays better than you do so that you'll have to work harder. You start playing your life with something bigger than you. You breathe hard. You're cycling up a huge hill. It hurts. Jesus is in pain in the garden before His arrest—"I am deeply troubled," He tells His friends. "So I want you to pray for me." They fall asleep. But He's very awake. He has grasped a purpose larger than His own needs. And it's very good. It's actually worth doing. Incubus sings a song called "Drive" about this process of becoming an active participant in the direction of your life without grasping or controlling:

> Sometimes, I feel the fear
> Of uncertainty, stinging clear.

And I can't help but ask myself
How much I'll let the fear
Take the wheel and steer ...
But lately I am beginning to find that I
Should be the one behind the wheel ...
Whatever tomorrow brings, I'll be there[10]

Truly letting go, releasing what the Buddhists call "attachment," is not about laziness or uselessness. It's the opposite. One of my heroes is my friend David. He is a fifty-year-old single dad of three teenage daughters, two of whom are in high school, and the other is in college. His wife left him ten years ago, and though he worked hard to repair his marriage, she decided she didn't love him anymore and that was that.

Over the years, he's done amazing things to be there for his daughters—even though he's also one of the ministers at my church, and a youth minister on top of that, which means he's available for a few hundred teenagers all the time, leading summer camps, going to football games, putting on Friday night worship services, and on and on and on. Wherever his wife moved over the years, he'd send his daughters to visit her, even driving them a few hundred and then driving back, and then making the loop again at the end of the visit. He coaches their ball games. He buys their prom dresses. And he will sit and listen to one of the high school students at our church for hours.

David is one of the most spiritually mature and compassionate people I've ever known. I've asked him how he's managed to survive over the years, and he smiles and shrugs and says, "It's just what you do." He hasn't dated. He says, "Right now, my job is to be there for my girls." He looks tired sometimes, but is almost always joyful. David

10 Boyd, Einziger, Katunich, Kilmore, and Pasillas, "Drive," Incubus, *Make Yourself*, c1999 EMI April Music Inc./ Hunglikeyora Music., c1999 Sony Music Entertainment Inc., 63652.

has figured something out. He is tied to something. He has loyalty to something worth living for. He's not bitter, although he carries his wounds and knows pain. But his wounds have become sacred wounds, and he is a healed person—not because he's perfect, but because he's in love with something worth living for. Ironically, he reminds me of my great-grandfather, who lived simply and provided for his family, and was content that that would be his life's meaning. The difference is, Granddaddy didn't know of any alternative. David's had any number of ways out, like all of us in the twenty-first century, but he keeps deciding to take up his cross, and let some things die, so that his heart will live. And it does. And because he is being healed, he is a mighty healer.

To embrace your struggle is to make it holy. To wrestle with God breaks us and heals us. It gives us a new name. It brings us back home—but not to the same mess we left. We're not that person anymore. To say, "Yes, this is where I am and who I am," is holy. It's where we are, and it's where God is as well. We meet God there. It surprises us—or not.

This is a mystery. It cannot be gotten or grasped. But it is available. It is not something you can buy or trade for or earn. It is also not something that will happen by itself. We will hear it; it will brush past us, if we are willing to allow some space for it, to get out of the way, to be still, to let darkness come. It turns out it's not darkness after all; the sun is coming up. We "step out in faith" as the saying goes, but not because when we arrive on the other side, we'll meet God. The other side isn't where God is.

This is the secret: God is in the step itself. I know the "we'll see" mind can accept this; I've seen it happen. Postmoderns are already hungry for this and prepared for it. But that doesn't make it easy. But it's still good. It's your journey. It belongs to you. Breathe it. Walk it.

DON'T BUILD YOUR CITY,
WALK YOUR RIVER

ONE LAST WORD

So, if God isn't what's on the other side of the step, but God is in the step, then what happens next? Don't you get to sit down and rest at some point?

When it was time to go on a family vacation when I was a kid, my stepfather liked for us to get up way before dawn and drive without stopping until we got to our destination. We'd be allowed a potty break if we were desperate. I can remember waking up in the back of the station wagon in my pajamas, with a blanket over me, somewhere in Arkansas, either headed away from or back toward home, the sun coming up or going down. I'm the opposite. Now that I have my own children, I drive them crazy because I just like to slow down, stop, and look around. It makes my wife nervous because I tend to look around *while* I'm driving, which I'll admit isn't necessarily smart. But I just love walking or driving. I adore riding horses, partly because I like horses a lot, but I think mostly because it's slow. I'm not trying to get away from anything or arrive anywhere; it just makes me happy to see what's out there.

I like to stop and walk through cemeteries, reading the headstones and thinking about the lives that have already been and are now over. There are a hundred million people's bones lying in layers all around us. They lived, just as we do, raising their children and working and taking care of whoever got sick. They played games. They were cruel to each other sometimes; sometimes they were charitable. Remembering that my own life isn't the first one, won't be the last one, and doesn't really matter all that much in any long-term sense, helps me keep perspective about my own silly little life—and reminds me that I'm just here for a little while. It's really liberating. I didn't feel that when I was a younger adult and wanted desperately to build my career and achieve something; my life seemed so short and I was in such a hurry. I didn't think I'd have enough time to get it all done. But when things didn't go my way, I began to slow down and shut up. It took me about a decade to even begin to stop being mad at God for not making me a corporate giant, movie star, rock and roll god, or NFL quarterback. I don't know what let it happen, but it happened: gradually, I looked around and, like George Bailey in *It's A Wonderful Life*, I began to realize just how incredibly lucky I am—and how little my plans and ambitions really matter after all. It soaked into my head about a year ago at Christmastime that Jimmy Stewart and Donna Reed and all the other adults who had been in that movie were now dead. They'd slipped off this mortal coil and were now spirits, seeing clearly what we here only see glimpses of. I longed for them, not only as they were in 1947, but as they are now, in the spirit space.

But to learn to be still and just be who you are, where you are, no matter what and where that is, is to get such a glimpse. I've been allowed to work being a teacher, and father, and husband. I still fight with it, though. I still want to matter. I still want to be an astronaut or have a washboard stomach. But it's occurring to me more and more: Be still. Be still. Look around. Look within.

Driving in the country during each season and paying attention to how it is different from the one before helps me remember that the landscape will be different in a month or two. So don't get too attached, but don't worry either.

This, by the way, is why I think it's a waste for Christians to obsess over wanting Jesus to come back soon and trying to predict when it will happen and why. It's pretty arrogant to think that all of the Old Testament and New Testament writers, the book of Revelation's strange symbolic codes, and Jesus himself, were all only thinking of the early part of the twenty-first century when they heard God speak about the coming of the renewal of all creation, and the coming of new heavens and the new earth. Jesus didn't seem particularly concerned about it; He seems in the texts to have suggested that whatever the next age would be, that it would happen soon after His death and resurrection. So did Paul, a generation later. But so far, the Christians are still waiting. The rest of the world is busy living. So we people of faith might as well raise some children, wash some feet, forgive each other, and feed the poor while we wait—and thereby usher in the presence of God.

During a trip to Colorado last year, we sat by a clear, powerful stream in the mountains outside Boulder one afternoon, with fast food joints and grocery stores a few miles below us. It occurred to me that a few decades before, people dressed like James Dean and Eleanor Roosevelt had walked up along this stream—and here it still was, coming down out of the cliffs above me. Then I thought of a group of people a hundred years ago who had stood by this stream and these mountains, and the mountain hasn't changed since. The Native Americans, a hundred years before that, had stood by these unmoving mountains as well. And before them, the mountains were still there, standing for thousands of years, losing a rock or two here, growing a shrub there. The fact that I happened to be standing there didn't matter to the mountain. And that thought, for some strange, not modern reason, felt really good. Making sure I had packed all the right CDs for the trip had very little to do with whether the joy of the Earth would or would not flow through that mountain stream.

I suggested earlier in this book that when you let go of so much you've been carrying—when you enter the desert and strip away your clothing, accomplishments, achievements, fears, even your created identity—you discover, in time, that you don't mind the journey. You travel easily. When you see all of life as a sacred journey rather than seeing yourself as lurching from one place and time to another, you're set free.

But, as the Renaissance explorers wrote on the edge of their maps, when you go further than you know about, there are probably dragons or monsters, or the end of the world. You find men you have to wrestle with in the dark. Tornados pick up your house and throw it. Mom used to say to us as we went out in the afternoons after school on our bikes, "Don't go too far! Stay where you can get home in time for supper! Don't stay out when it gets too dark!" We still think that'd be best, only now it's about our spirits. Let's not travel. It's too dangerous. There might be dragons. Let's just build a nice house/ empire/ business/ life here. Let's just build our city.

And yet I know that the twenty-first century mind doesn't want that at all. What it wants is some freedom; it already *has* freedom. We live in a time when we can make our own decisions. We're not like the generation before us who came of age in the sixties and seventies. They had the burden of wrestling their culture free from the strong arms of their parents, the Builder generation who had made it through the massive industrialization of America, and the growth of cities, and the Depression, and World War II, and were about to hand over all of that progress and weight to their children. So when the hippies and revolutionaries and civil rights workers and musicians and everyday folks tried to push the pendulum the other direction and ask tough questions, the pendulum's inertia was so strong that they couldn't get it to go very far. To my grandmother, it seemed like the world was falling apart in 1969, but looking back, I can see that things were only beginning to change. Thirty years later, we're much more free. Our parents don't have all that heritage to harness onto our shoulders; they took it apart. So, we are actually free to start on our own. We can choose what we want.

In our best moments, those of us with a "we'll see" mind realize that to build a city or a fortress would be settling for less. And it is.

In the healthy, healing life, wrestling with God doesn't stop. Jacob's—Israel's—life doesn't end when he returns home; there's a whole Bible that follows after that. And it's not all happy stories, even though his reunion with his brother Esau is full of forgiveness and acceptance. Eventually, Jacob/ Israel's story becomes the story of an entire people who continue throughout the Bible to wrestle with who they are and who God is—and in that story they are a small family who represent all of humanity. Throughout all the generations, all the violence, all the messed-up marriages, all the separation and restoration, all the discoveries and losses, there is God. That's the message. God is present. God is part of the struggle. God is in every journey.

Emily Dickinson said that when she had read what she called "a true poem"—one that tells the truth about the human experience, one that doesn't flinch, one that is wrestling—"It is as if I feel that the top of my head is coming off." That's spirit space. That's prayer. That's the journey. That's when you get next to a mountain and realize how little you are—and yet that you, too, are part of that story. You aren't little anymore; that's the weird part. You're big—because you can just be still. You contain multitudes.

I saw Bill Gates on television talking about taking a trip to India to figure out ways to help improve health care in the developing world. He talked about how he wants to give so much of his money away and about how having three children had expanded his sense of who he was and what life was about. Bill Gates. Multi-billionaire. Bruce Wayne. The head of one of the largest companies ever in the history of the world. And yet, changing diapers and caring for the sick is what is making him feel like a real human being. Amazing. And right.

Life Is Short, So Move Slowly

San Antonio poet Naomi Shihab Nye said, "Life is so short, we must move very slowly." Our hearts yearn for silence—what Nye refers to as poetry and others refer to as peace, silence, truth, prayer, recovery, the spiritual life, salvation, especially those of us who are young enough to be disinterested in and unbound by the values and memories of the good old days. We hunger for some new days—and not just new things, but a new way to live.

Yet, as the earlier chapter in this book says, you have to trust something. And to slow down requires trust. As long as we are like the young Jacob, frantically running around, afraid we won't be enough, we won't have our own blessing, we won't achieve what we're desperate for, then we can't possibly slow down. As long as we're building our empire and running through husbands and phases, being still is not an option. Yet most amazing things are small and still, things you will only notice if you slow down along your journey and study the surface of the river and the rocks. Most lasting things aren't particularly flashy or sexy. This goes against our culture, but then you knew that already. The issue is making the choice between the two.

Jesus is never in a hurry. He's the Son of God who has only three years to communicate a message that can remake all of humanity. Yet when the disciples want Him to hurry, He goes slower. He interrupts His own important public addresses to play with children. If the crowds are growing and His campaign is getting some good momentum going and His lieutenants want Him to make a political or religious icon, He tells them that they all need to be ready to die. Most of them leave. Instead of building His empire, He sits with His friends and eats and talks. He listens to people. And when it's time to be alone, He disappears and doesn't tell anyone where He's going. His spiritual life is His empire.

Your life isn't a map or a timeline. It isn't a resume. It isn't a report. It's a story. It's a story that loops back onto itself, refuses to make sense, goes off track, speeds up, stops, turns crazy corners, and then somehow ends up in death—regardless of how it got there. If the point of our lives is to get from one thing to another, no wonder we're in a hurry. Why would we want to slow down? All you end up is dead anyway.

But if our lives aren't about arriving anywhere, then everything is part of the story. There isn't a happy or a sad ending. After all, if it's not about arriving, it doesn't end. God doesn't go in any order and neither does your soul. So just accept that.

Slow down. Pay attention. Be still. Turn off an electronic device for a while. Go alone into the desert when the Spirit sends you there, but don't try to make it happen. And when you go, don't be afraid. God is with you.

Learn to give up your answers and your control. You don't need your weapons. They won't work anyway—at least, not forever. All that will ultimately work is trusting something larger than you are. That something is God, the Spirit, love.

Don't seek to be broken, but don't run from brokenness. Let it come when it needs to. Listen and see what it does in you.

Tell yourself the truth—especially if it hurts. Don't kid yourself. Don't settle for half-truth. Grow stronger. You can take it.

Don't arrive.

Celebrate.

Keep walking, even if you're limping.

Carry your new name and your wounds.

God is with you. You are enough. Keep wrestling. Let go, hang on. Do whatever you are called to do; or do nothing. Be still. Just keep walking.

ALSO FROM RELEVANT BOOKS

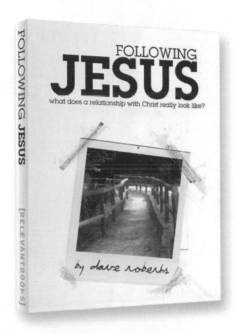

RED MOON RISING
How 24-7 Prayer is
Awakening a Generation

FOLLOWING JESUS
What Does A Relationship
With Christ Really Look Like

Available at retailers nationwide
or online at www.RELEVANTbooks.com

[RELEVANTBOOKS]